MOTHER MARIA
SKOBTSOVA

☦

MODERN SPIRITUAL MASTERS
Robert Ellsberg, Series Editor

This series introduces the writing and vision of some of the great spiritual masters of the twentieth century. Along with selections from their writings, each volume includes a comprehensive introduction, presenting the author's life and writings in context and drawing attention to points of special relevance to contemporary spirituality.

Some of these authors found a wide audience in their lifetimes. In other cases recognition has come long after their deaths. Some are rooted in long-established traditions of spirituality. Others charted new, untested paths. In each case, however, the authors in this series have engaged in a spiritual journey shaped by the influences and concerns of our age. Such concerns include the challenges of modern science, religious pluralism, secularism, and the quest for social justice.

At the dawn of a new millennium this series commends these modern spiritual masters, along with the saints and witnesses of previous centuries, as guides and companions to a new generation of seekers.

Already published:
Dietrich Bonhoeffer (edited by Robert Coles)
Simone Weil (edited by Eric O. Springsted)
Henri Nouwen (edited by Robert A. Jonas)
Pierre Teilhard de Chardin (edited by Ursula King)
Anthony de Mello (edited by William Dych, S.J.)
Charles de Foucauld (edited by Robert Ellsberg)
Oscar Romero (by Marie Dennis, Rennie Golden,
    and Scott Wright)
Eberhard Arnold (edited by Johann Christoph Arnold)
Thomas Merton (edited by Christine M. Bochen)
Thich Nhat Hanh (edited by Robert Ellsberg)
Rufus Jones (edited by Kerry Walters)
Mother Teresa (edited by Jean Maalouf)
Edith Stein (edited by John Sullivan, O.C.D.)
John Main (edited by Laurence Freeman)
Mohandas Gandhi (edited by John Dear)
Evelyn Underhill (edited by Emilie Griffin)

MODERN SPIRITUAL MASTERS SERIES

MOTHER MARIA
SKOBTSOVA

Essential Writings

Translated from the Russian by
RICHARD PEVEAR
and
LARISSA VOLOKHONSKY

Introduction by
JIM FOREST

ORBIS BOOKS

Maryknoll, New York 10545

Founded in 1970, Orbis Books endeavors to publish works that enlighten the mind, nourish the spirit, and challenge the conscience. The publishing arm of the Maryknoll Fathers and Brothers, Orbis seeks to explore the global dimensions of the Christian faith and mission, to invite dialogue with diverse cultures and religious traditions, and to serve the cause of reconciliation and peace. The books published reflect the views of their authors and do not represent the official position of the Maryknoll Society. To learn more about Maryknoll and Orbis Books, please visit our website at www.maryknoll.org.

Originally published in French under the title *Le Sacrement du Frère* by Mère Marie Skobtsov, © 1995 by Editions Le Sel de la Terre, 79, Avenue C.-F. Ramuz, CH-1009 Pully, Switzerland. The present expanded edition is translated from the original Russian texts. The translation of "Types of Religious Life" is by Fr. Alvian Smirensky and Elisabeth Obolensky. It is reprinted with permission of *Sourozh*, the diocesan journal of the Russian Orthodox Church in Britain. The publisher thanks Dr. Michael Plekon for preparing introductory notes to the essays of Mother Maria Skobtsova and for otherwise facilitating this publication. Special thanks are also due to Hélène Klepinin-Arjakovsky for her role in preserving the work and memory of Mother Maria Skobtsova and for her cooperation with this edition.

Manufactured in the United States of America

Library of Congress Cataloging-in-Publication Data
Maria, Mother, 1891–1945.
  [Selections. English. 2002]
  Mother Maria Skobtsova : essential writings / introduction by Jim Forest ; translated from the Russian by Richard Pevear and Larissa Volokhonsky.
    p. cm. – (Modern spiritual masters series)
  ISBN 1-57075-436-5 (pbk.)
  1. Spiritual life. 2. Maria, Mother, 1891–1945. I. Pevear, Richard, 1943- II. Volokhonsky, Larissa. III. Maria, Mother, 1891-1945. Sacrement du frère. IV. Title. V. Series.
BV4501.3 .M2613 2002
281.9 – dc21

                                              2002005036

Contents

Preface
by Olivier Clément

Mother Maria died at Ravensbrück over fifty years ago. Did she take the place of another woman selected for the crematory's oven or was she sent there by chance? Even the facts of her death are unknown to the hagiographers. She had always hoped to be able to survive in order to undertake the work made possible by the war — to bring about a genuine *rapprochement* between Russia and the West. During the last weeks of her life, she traded her bread for thread and began to embroider an unusual icon of the Mother of God carrying a crucified Jesus in her arms.

Many people saw the life of Mother Maria as one long scandal. This former socialist revolutionary, twice married, became a Christian without ever having stopped being the socialist revolutionary, an intellectual of leftist bent. She was an anarchist even in her dress. Her revolutionary sympathies and her love for the Jews shocked not only rightist Russian emigrants but also many young Orthodox Christians who longed for an order that was complete, organic, and sacred.

This nun, who denounced most monasteries as mediocre substitutes for family life, scandalized many committed to solitary contemplation and carrying out the "works of God." For Maria, it was a matter of renouncing all comfort — whether it was a soothing liturgy or the peace of a cloister — to completely dedicate herself to a life of poverty and love for others. She immersed herself in a form of abasement similar to the abasement of God, who became human because of love.

Her immense, forceful, and passionate vitality expressed itself in a surge of love. Her love was not increasingly calm, but crucified; it expanded into infinity and was transformed into spiritual motherhood. Indeed, as a revolutionary young girl she already acted as a mother. She protected poor students in Yalta from the police and taught laborers in St. Petersburg how to read. When she was only eighteen, following a totally illogical impulse, she married an intellectual revolutionary to save him from alcoholism and failure.

Her second marriage, begun during the civil war, seemed to have been based on pure passion and her desire for protection. But soon her role as mother was wounded by the death of her beloved daughter, Liza. However, she would again get the upper hand and find the meaning of her suffering in the second commandment of the Gospel — to love one's neighbor. "I feel that the death of my child obliges me to become the mother of everyone," she wrote. Later she would see the prototype of this love in the love of the Mother of God at the foot of the cross, contemplating both her son and her God in the Crucified Jesus. In the same way, she said, we have to discern in the face of everyone both the image of God and of the Son who was so compassionately given to us. This was the theme of her last icon at Ravensbrück.

"My feelings for everyone are maternal," wrote Mother Maria. This included the stevedores of Marseilles, the iron miners in the Pyrenees, the mentally ill, and the drug addicts and alcoholics that she hunted out in their nighttime hovels and took home to soothe like babies. She cared for everyone, including the persecuted Jews marked with the yellow Star of David and her other companions at Ravensbrück. Faced with so much distress, she had no time for distinctions between love of neighbor and love of those far away, or between concrete acts of charity between two people and organized programs of social action.

For Mother Maria it was not necessary to choose between one or the other; instead she added on and multiplied her love. Love was not to be divided. Although she wanted to love each human being as a son or daughter, she also knew how to organize effectively, whether it be Orthodox Action, with its houses of hospitality and its networks of friends, or the pacifist struggle of spiritual resistance during the occupation, or even the humble study circles in concentration camps where prisoners found once again the taste of beauty and free expression and felt themselves completely free.

Mother Maria was part of the great Orthodox tradition that demonstrated love for neighbor to the point of total abandon, as did Christ. The Orthodox monastic tradition is centered on a form of solitary contemplation that consumes the practitioner in obeying the first commandment — to love God with one's heart, soul, and mind so to become a pillar of intercession linking together earth and heaven; the practitioner's only purpose is to be a secret blessing for the world and the universe. This total dedication was sometimes manifested in the charismatic ministry of the *starets* (monastic spiritual directors).

This ascetic tradition, however, is constantly threatened by pride and by a loss of sensitivity to others, by making idols of spiritual states and abilities, and by contempt for ordinary life and the world. The tradition is also in danger of installing itself in the peace and equilibrium of a monasticism that isolates itself from the love of the world and any spiritual struggle. This is why God has never ceased questioning this tradition, testing it, indeed humiliating it, in order to produce witnesses — simple or inspired, but always creators of life — of a total love of neighbor.

The lives of the Desert Fathers often show Christ himself sending the purest ascetics to learn from a laborer or a mother or a thief who, living as human beings among other human beings, would know how to truly love their neighbor. Humility, freedom, and the wild spontaneity of love that refuses any form of hypocrisy — these are the trademarks of the "foolishness of Christ." In sixteenth-century Russia, these "fools" often had a prophetic message and intervened without hesitation in political or civic affairs. Mother Maria consciously placed herself well within this tradition.

The texts included in this book demonstrate these preferences of Mother Maria. She lived a theology of encounter like that expressed in Matthew 25 with the simple resolve of a Dietrich Bonhoeffer. Like him, she engaged herself fully in history, in organized spiritual resistance that she refused to distinguish from military resistance. But she remained fundamentally Orthodox in her mystical fervor and her love for the crucified and risen Christ, in her understanding of the cross of glory as the central point of history, and in her openness to the dynamism of the Holy Spirit.

Other signs of her Orthodoxy were her suffering, her sighs, her indescribable laments, and her ascetic discipline. Mother Maria knew well that impartial love of neighbor may uncover the image not only of God but also of the devil. For that reason she was aware that an authentic encounter was not the same as a true "sacrament of fellowship"; for that, the powerful exorcism of the Church and the most difficult spiritual struggle were necessary. This is why an ascetical practice of human encounter, as she sketched it as part of her study of the second commandment, is a significant resource for Christian thought today.

Located at the center of the spiritual history of Orthodox Christianity, the life of Mother Maria serves as both summary and prophecy. Pobedonostsev, the redoubtable procurer of the Holy Synod, with whom she corresponded as a child, had taught her the love of neighbor as opposed to love of those far away; she discovered that she loved individual human beings as opposed to humanity. Revolutionaries taught her love of the human race; the revolution showed her that the revolutionaries loved humanity instead of the individual person. While the Russian literary renaissance gave her a taste for the spiritual — even as a revolutionary she was never materialistic — it was an anemic spirituality, without any real engagement with life or any power to change social situations.

This is why Mother Maria calls us to use the richness of our various charisms to move beyond our fears and differences in order to achieve a totality of love, love that does not neglect either the material or social conditions of humankind. Mother Maria, who did not preach but loved, never forgot that the only thing of real value is that which makes human beings more like the image of God they bear. This is a prophetic testimony for the future of the Orthodox faith.

The life and death of Mother Maria are also prophetic for us Orthodox in the West, especially for all young people who seek love and are willing to take a chance, but who no longer know where to find God. According to Mother Maria, God is in the center, God is in the heart of human beings and things, in the very density of the material world, in suffering, and in our shared creation. In 1915, through the work of the Indian poet Tagore, she had become totally aware of the sovereign power of the second commandment. The Church is nothing other than the world on the way to deification; for the Church, the world is no longer a tomb, but a womb.

This transfiguration of the world requires creative contemplation, active love, the most heartrending personal compassion, and the ability to reinvent life. It is a question of giving human beings not only bread, but also beauty, opportunity, and celebration.

We should not forget that Mother Maria knew how to create these privileged spaces where life was lived and embraced. She embellished these spaces with icons and tapestries. She wrote continually — poetry, but also real mystery plays that were never performed. She was not an activist but a poet of life, always at the center of the creative space where her "holiness and genius" were played out.

The life of Mother Maria underlines the extraordinary diversity of the Orthodox faith. It also poses a real problem both today and in the future for the Orthodox Church — that is the need for new forms of monastic life in which the second commandment would occupy the central place.

Mother Maria wanted to become a nun, not to take on the monastic tradition of becoming a hermit or cenobite (less the former than the latter), but to manifest her commitment with no turning back. She was determined to consecrate herself and give herself totally. Inevitably, she found herself in contradiction with traditional attitudes. Is it possible for us to realize what she desired?

When Metropolitan Evlogy received her monastic profession, he gave her the ascetic assignment of the "desert of the human heart." What Mother Maria sought, but with more vehemence and creative energy, was an acute and nearly anarchic awareness of the freedom of the Holy Spirit. This is to some extent what

Western Christianity has sought over a long period of time in small charismatic communities. Is not this a call for us today?

Beside the traditions of those vowed to and nourished by silence, are we not in need of great creators of love and life to labor and make fertile the desert of our souls?

One last word. If we love and venerate Mother Maria, it is not in spite of her disorder, her strange views, and her passions. It is precisely these qualities that make her extraordinarily alive among so many bland and pious saints. Unattractive and dirty, strong, thick, and sturdy, yes, she was truly alive in her suffering, her compassion, her passion.

— *Translated by Susan Perry*

Introduction

Mother Maria of Paris

by Jim Forest

> *"No amount of thought will ever result in any greater for-mulation than the three words, 'Love one another,' so long as it is love to the end and without exceptions."*

Though Mother Maria Skobtsova is not yet formally canonized, those who know the details of her life tend to regard her as one of the great saints of the twentieth century: a brilliant theo-logian who lived her faith bravely in nightmarish times, finally dying a martyr's death at the Ravensbrück concentration camp in Germany in 1945.

No one knows how many lives this Russian-born nun saved in France during the German occupation — hundreds, certainly, perhaps thousands. She never counted.

In the decades since she died, many books by or about her have been published, but only two in English. There have been several plays and a film, but none of these have yet reached audiences beyond the French- and Russian-speaking worlds.

Like America's Dorothy Day, she embraced a vocation of hospitality, but in Mother Maria's case it was finally illegal hos-pitality in a world under Nazi rule. Her arrest and eventual death were the result of rescuing Jews and others in danger in the Hitler years.

Yet little by little her life and theological reflections are reach-ing the wider world. Now we have this impressive collection of Mother Maria's essays, all but one of which are translations by Richard Pevear and Larissa Volokhonsky, renowned for their new editions of Dostoevsky, Gogol, and Tolstoy.

13

This sampling of Mother Maria's writings was gathered by Hélène Klepinin-Arjakovsky, herself intimately linked to Mother Maria. Hélène is the granddaughter of Father Dimitri Klepinin, a priest who worked side by side with Mother Maria and also died in a Nazi concentration camp. It is thanks to Hélène that the final essay in this collection, "Types of Religious Life," was discovered only a few years ago. Apparently it was a text Mother Maria was working on in the last months before her arrest.

While it was in France and Germany that Mother Maria made the choices for which she will best be remembered, she was a Russian by birth and finally a nun of the Russian Orthodox Church.

Elizaveta Pilenko, the future Mother Maria, was born in 1891 in the Latvian city of Riga, then part of the Russian Empire, and grew up in the south of Russia on a family estate near the town of Anapa on the shore of the Black Sea.[1] In her family she was known as Liza. For a time her father was mayor of Anapa. Later he was director of a botanical garden and school at Yalta. On her mother's side, Liza was descended from the last governor of the Bastille, the Parisian prison destroyed during the French Revolution.

Her parents were devout Orthodox Christians, whose faith helped shape their daughter's values, sensitivities, and goals. As a child she once emptied her piggy bank in order to contribute to the painting of an icon that would be part of a new church in Anapa. At seven she asked her mother if she was old enough to become a nun, while a year later she sought permission to become a pilgrim to spend her life walking from shrine to shrine. (As late as 1940, when living in German-occupied Paris, thoughts of one day being a wandering pilgrim and missionary in Siberia again filled her imagination.)

When she was fourteen, her father died, an event that seemed to her meaningless and unjust and led her to atheism. "If there is no justice," she said, "there is no God." She decided God's nonexistence was well known to adults but kept secret from children. For her, childhood was over.

When her widowed mother moved the family to St. Petersburg in 1906, she found herself in the country's political and cultural center — also a hotbed of radical ideas and groups.

She became part of radical literary circles that gathered around such symbolist poets as Alexander Blok, whom she first met at age fifteen. Blok responded to their unexpected meeting — Liza had come to visit unannounced — with a poem that included the lines:

> Only someone who is in love
> Has the right to call himself a human being.

In a note that came with the poem, Blok told Liza that many people were dying where they stood. The world-weary poet urged her "to run, run from us, the dying ones." She replied with a vow to fight "against death and against wickedness."

Like so many of her contemporaries, she was drawn to the left, but was often disappointed with the radicals she encountered. Though regarding themselves as revolutionaries, they seemed to do nothing but talk. "My spirit longed to engage in heroic feats, even to perish, to combat the injustice of the world," she recalled. Yet none of those she knew were actually laying down their life for others. Should her friends hear of someone dying for the Revolution, she noted, "they will value it, approve or not approve, show understanding on a very high level, and discuss the night away till the sun rises and it's time for fried eggs. But they will not understand at all that to die for the Revolution means to feel a rope around one's neck."

Liza began teaching evening courses to workers at the Poutilov Plant, but later gave it up in disillusionment when one of her students told her that he and his classmates weren't interested in learning as such, but saw classes as a necessary path to becoming clerks and bureaucrats. The teenage Liza wanted her workers to be every bit as idealistic as she was.

In 1910, Liza married Dimitri Kuzmin-Karaviev, a member of the Social Democrat Party, better known as the Bolsheviks. She was eighteen; he was twenty-one. It was a marriage born "more of pity than of love," she later commented. Dimitri had spent a short time in prison several years before, but by the time of their marriage was part of a community of poets, artists, and writers in which it was normal to rise at three in the afternoon and talk the night through until dawn. She not only knew poets but also wrote poems in the symbolist mode. In 1912 her first collection of poetry, *Scythian Shards,* was published.

Like many other Russian intellectuals, she later reflected, she was a participant in the revolution before the Revolution that was "so deeply, pitilessly and fatally laid over the soil of old traditions" only to destroy far more than it created. "Such courageous bridges we erected to the future! At the same time, this depth and courage were combined with a kind of decay, with the spirit of dying, of ghostliness, ephemerality. We were in the last act of the tragedy, the rupture between the people and the intelligentsia."

She and her friends also talked theology, but just as their political ideas had no connection at all to the lives of ordinary people, their theology floated far above the actual Church. There was much they might have learned, she reflected later in life, from "any old beggar woman hard at her Sunday prostrations in church." For many intellectuals, the Church was an idea or a set of abstract values, not a community in which one actually lives.

Though she still regarded herself as an atheist, little by little her earlier attraction to Christ revived and deepened, not yet Christ as God incarnate but Christ as heroic man. "Not for God, for He does not exist, but for the Christ," she said. "He also died. He sweated blood. They struck His face...[while] we pass by and touch His wounds and yet are not burned by His blood."

One door opened to another. Liza found herself drawn toward the religious faith she had jettisoned after her father's death. She prayed and read the Gospel and the lives of saints. It seemed to her that the real need of the people was not for revolutionary theories but for Christ. She wanted "to proclaim the simple word of God," she told Blok in a letter written in 1916. The same year her second collection of poems, *Ruth,* appeared in St. Petersburg.

Deciding to study theology, she applied for entrance to the Theological Academy of the Alexander Nevsky Monastery in

St. Petersburg, in those days an entirely male school whose students were preparing for ordination as priests. As surprising as her wanting to study there was the rector's decision that she could be admitted.

By 1913, Liza's marriage collapsed. (Later in his life Dimitri became a Christian, joined the Catholic Church, and later lived and worked among Jesuits in Western Europe.) That October her first child, Gaiana, was born.

Just as World War I was beginning, Liza returned with her daughter to her family's country home near Anapa in Russia's deep south. Her religious life became more intense. For a time she secretly wore lead weights sewn into a hidden belt as a way of reminding herself both "that Christ exists" and also to be more aware that minute-by-minute many people were suffering and dying in the war. She realized, however, that the primary goal of Christian asceticism was not self-mortification, but caring response to the needs of other people while at the same time trying to create better social structures. She joined the ill-fated Social Revolutionary Party, a movement that, despite the contrast in names, was far more democratic than Lenin's Social Democratic Party.

On a return visit to St. Petersburg, Liza spent hours visiting a small chapel best known for a healing icon in which small coins had been embedded when lightning struck the poor box that stood nearby — it was called the Mother of God, Joy of the Sorrowful, with Kopeks. Here she prayed in a dark corner, reviewing her life as one might prepare for confession, finally feeling God's overwhelming presence. "God is over all," she knew with certainty, "unique and expiating everything."

In October 1917, Liza was present in St. Petersburg when Russia's provisional government was overthrown by the Bolsheviks. Taking part in the All-Russian Soviet Congress, she heard Lenin's lieutenant, Leon Trotsky, dismiss people from her party with the words, "Your role is played out. Go where you belong, into history's garbage can!"

On the way home, she narrowly escaped summary execution by convincing a Bolshevik sailor that she was a friend of Lenin's wife. It was on that difficult journey of many train rides and long waits at train stations that she began to see the scale of the catastrophe Russia was now facing: terror, random murder, massacres, destroyed villages, the rule of hooligans and thugs, hunger and massive dislocation. How hideously different actual revolution was from the dreams of revolution that had once filled the imagination of so many Russians, not least the intellectuals!

In February 1918, in the early days of Russia's civil war, Liza was elected deputy mayor of Anapa. She hoped she could keep the town's essential services working and protect anyone in danger of the firing squad. "The fact of having a female mayor," she noted, "was seen as something obviously revolutionary." Thus they put up with "views that would not have been tolerated from any male."

She became acting mayor after the town's Bolshevik mayor fled when the White Army took control of the region. Again her life was in danger. To the White forces, Liza looked as Red as any Bolshevik. She was arrested, jailed, and put on trial for collaboration with the enemy. In court, she rose and spoke in her own defense: "My loyalty was not to any imagined government as such, but to those whose need of justice was greatest, the people. Red or White, my position is the same — I will act for justice and for the relief of suffering. I will try to love my neighbor."

It was thanks to Daniel Skobtsov, a former schoolmaster who was now her judge, that Liza avoided execution. After the trial, she sought him out to thank him. They fell in love and within days were married. Before long Liza once again found herself pregnant.

The tide of the civil war was now turning in favor of the Bolsheviks. Both Liza and her husband were in peril, as well as her daughter and unborn child. They made the decision many thousands were making: it was safest to go abroad. Liza's mother, Sophia, came with them.

Their journey took them across the Black Sea to Georgia in the putrid hold of a storm-beaten steamer. Liza's son Yura was born in Tbilisi in 1920. A year later they left for Istanbul and from there traveled to Yugoslavia, where Liza gave birth to Anastasia, or Nastia as she was called in the family.

Their long journey finally ended in France. They arrived in Paris in 1923. Friends gave them use of a room. Daniel found work as a part-time teacher, though the job paid too little to cover expenses. To supplement their income, Liza made dolls and painted silk scarves, often working ten or twelve hours a day.

A friend introduced her to the Russian Student Christian Movement (SCM), an Orthodox association founded in Paris in 1923. Liza began attending lectures and taking part in other activities of the group. She felt herself coming back to life spiritually and intellectually.

In the hard winter of 1926, each person in the family came down with influenza. All recovered except Nastia, who became thinner with each passing day. At last a doctor diagnosed meningitis. The Pasteur Institute accepted Nastia as a patient, also giving Liza permission to stay day and night to help care for her daughter.

Liza's vigil was to no avail. After a month in the hospital, Nastia died. Even then, for a day and night, her grief-stricken mother sat by Nastia's side, unable to leave the room. During those desolate hours, she came to feel how she had never known "the meaning of repentance, but now I am aghast at my own insignificance.... I feel that my soul has meandered down back alleys all my life. And now I want an authentic and purified road. Not out of faith in life, but in order to justify, understand, and accept death.... No amount of thought will ever result in any greater formulation than the three words, 'Love one another,' so long as it is love to the end and without exceptions. And then the whole of life is illumined, which is otherwise an abomination and a burden."

When someone you love has died, she wrote, "the gates have suddenly opened onto eternity, all natural life has trembled and collapsed, yesterday's laws have been abolished, desires have faded, meaning has become meaningless, and another incomprehensible Meaning has grown wings on their backs.... Everything

flies into the black maw of the fresh grave: hopes, plans, calculations, and, above all, meaning, the meaning of a whole life. If this
is so, then everything has to be reconsidered, everything rejected,
seen in its corruptibility and falseness."

After her daughter's burial, Liza became "aware of a new
and special, broad and all-embracing motherhood." She emerged
from her mourning with a determination to seek "a more authentic and purified life." She felt she saw a "new road before me and
a new meaning in life, to be a mother for all, for all who need
maternal care, assistance, or protection."

Liza devoted herself more and more to social work and theological writing with a social emphasis. In 1927 two volumes,
Harvest of the Spirit, were published, in which she retold the
lives of many saints.

In the same period, her husband began driving a taxi, a job
that provided a better income than part-time teaching. By now
Gaiana was living at a boarding school in Belgium, thanks to
help from her father. But Liza and Daniel's marriage was dying,
perhaps a casualty of Nastia's death.

Feeling driven to devote herself as fully as possible to social
service, Liza, with her mother, moved to central Paris, thus closer
to her work. It was agreed that Yura would remain with his father, though always free to visit and stay with his mother, until he
was fourteen, when he would decide for himself with which par-
ent he would live. (In fact Yura, found to be in the early stages of
tuberculosis, was to spend a lengthy period in a sanitarium apart
from both parents.)

In 1930, the same year her third book of poetry was published,
Liza was appointed traveling secretary of the SCM, work which
put her into daily contact with impoverished Russian refugees in
cities, towns, and villages throughout France and sometimes in
neighboring countries.

After completing a lecture in some provincial center, Liza
might afterward find herself involved in confessional conversations with those who had come to hear her and who sensed that
she was something more than an intellectual with a suitcase full

of ideas and theories. "We would embark on frank conversations about émigré life or else about the past. . . . A queue would form by the door as if outside a confessional. There would be people wanting to pour out their hearts, to tell of some terrible grief which had burdened them for years, of pangs of conscience which gave them no peace."

She took literally Christ's words that he was always present in the least person. "A person should have a more attentive attitude toward his brother's flesh than toward his own," she wrote. "Christian love teaches us to give our brother not only material but also spiritual gifts. We must give him our last shirt and our last crust of bread. Here personal charity is as necessary and justified as the broadest social work."

"In turning his spiritual world toward the spiritual world of another," she reflected,

> a man encounters the terrible, inspiring mystery. . . . He encounters . . . the authentic image of God in man, the very incarnate icon of God in the world, a glimmer of the mystery of the Incarnation and Godmanhood.[2] And man must unconditionally and unreservedly accept this terrible Revelation of God, must bow down before the image of God in his brother. And only when he feels it, sees it, and understands it, will yet another mystery be revealed to him, which demands of him his most strenuous struggle. . . . He will see how this image of God is obscured, distorted by an evil power. . . . In the name of the love for this image of God that pierces his heart, he will want to begin a struggle with the devil.

While the work suited her, the question of her true vocation was still unsettled in her life. She began to envision a new type of community, "half monastic and half fraternal," which would connect spiritual life with service to those in need, in the process showing "that a free Church can perform miracles."

Metropolitan Anthony, now the Russian Orthodox bishop in London, then a layman in Paris, where he was studying to become a physician, recalls a story about her from this period that he heard from a friend:

> [S]he went to the steel foundry in Creusot, where a large number of Russian [refugees] were working. She came there and announced that she was preparing to give a series of lectures on Dostoevsky. She was met with general howling: "We do not need Dostoevsky. We need linen ironed, we need our rooms cleaned, we need our clothes mended — and you bring us Dostoevsky!" And she answered: "Fine, if that is needed, let us leave Dostoevsky alone." And for several days she cleaned rooms, sewed, mended, ironed, cleaned. When she had finished doing all that, they asked her to talk about Dostoevsky. This made a big impression on me, because she did not say: "I did not come here to iron for you or clean your rooms. Can you not do that yourselves?" She responded immediately, and in this way she won the hearts and minds of the people.

Father Sergei Bulgakov, her confessor, was a source of support and encouragement. He had been a Marxist economist before his conversion to Orthodox Christianity. In 1918 he was ordained to the priesthood in Moscow and then five years later was expelled from the USSR. He settled in Paris and became dean at the newly founded St. Sergius Theological Institute. A spiritual father to many people, he was a confessor who respected the freedom of all who sought his guidance, never demanding obedience, never manipulating.

She also had a supportive bishop, Metropolitan Evlogy Georgievsky. From 1921 to 1946 he was responsible for the spiritual care of many thousands of Russian expatriates scattered across Europe, with the greatest concentration in France. "Everyone had access to him," recalled Father Lev Gillet, "and placed on his shoulders all the spiritual or material burdens....He wanted to give everyone the possibility of following his or her own call." Metropolitan Evlogy had become aware of Liza through her social work and was the first one to suggest to her the possibility of becoming a nun.

Assured she would be free to develop a new type of monasticism, engaged in the world and marked by the "complete absence of even the subtlest barrier which might separate the heart from the world and its wounds," Liza said she was willing to take such a step, but there was the obvious problem of her being married, even if now living alone. For a time it seemed the obstacles were insurmountable, as Daniel Skobtsov did not approve of his estranged wife taking monastic vows, but he changed his mind after Metropolitan Evlogy came to meet him. An ecclesiastical divorce was issued on March 7, 1932. A few weeks later, in the chapel at St. Sergius Theological Institute, Liza was professed as a nun. She was given the name Maria. She made her monastic profession, Metropolitan Evlogy recognized, "in order to give herself unreservedly to social service." Mother Maria called it simply "monasticism in the world."

From the beginning Mother Maria's intention was "to share the life of paupers and tramps," but exactly how she would do that wasn't yet clear to her. She lived in a room made available to her by Lev and Valentina Zander as she contemplated the next step in her life.

That summer on behalf of the Russian SCM she set out to visit Estonia and Latvia, where, in contrast to Soviet Russia, convents and monasteries still flourished. Here she had a first-hand experience of traditional monastic life. The experience strengthened her conviction that her own vocation must follow a different path. It seemed to her that no one in the monasteries she visited was aware that "the world is on fire" or sensed that the times cried out for a new form of monasticism. In a time of massive social disruption, she wrote, it was better to offer a monastic witness which opened its gates to the desperate people living outside and in so doing participate in Christ's self-abasement. "And I think that anyone who has at least once felt himself in this eternity, has at least once realized what path he is following, has seen at least once the One who walks ahead of him, will find it hard to turn from this path; to him all coziness will seem flimsy, all riches without value, all companions unnecessary, if he does not see among them the one Companion bearing the cross."

It was clear to her that it was not only Russia that was being torn to shreds:

> There are times when all that has been said cannot be made obvious and clear since the atmosphere around us is a pagan one and we are tempted by its idolatrous charms. But our times are firmly in tune with Christianity in that suffering is part of their nature. They demolish and destroy in our hearts all that is stable, mature, hallowed by the ages and treasured by us. They help us genuinely and utterly to accept the vows of poverty, to seek no rule, but rather anarchy, the anarchic life of Fools for Christ's sake, seeking no monastic enclosure, but the complete absence of even the subtlest barrier which might separate the heart from the world and its wounds.

Mother Maria had a particular devotion to saints who were classed as Holy Fools: people who behaved outrageously and yet revealed Christ in a remarkable way — such Holy Fools as St. Basil the Blessed, whose feast on August 2 she kept with special attentiveness. An icon she painted contains scenes from his life. The Holy Fools were, she wrote, saints of freedom. "Freedom calls us, contrary to the whole world, contrary not only to the pagans but to many who style themselves Christians, to undertake the Church's work in what is precisely the most difficult way. And we will become fools in Christ, because we know not only the difficulty of this path but also the immense happiness of feeling God's hand upon what we do."[3]

She saw that there were two ways to live. The first was on dry land, a legitimate and respectable place to be, where one could measure, weigh, and plan ahead. The second was to walk on the waters where "it becomes impossible to measure or plan ahead. The one thing necessary is to believe all the time. If you doubt for an instant, you begin to sink."

The water she decided to travel on was a vocation of welcoming and caring for those in desperate need. She began to look for a house of hospitality and found it at 9 villa de Saxe in Paris.

Metropolitan Evlogy remained deeply committed to Mother Maria's activities. When she had to sign the lease and had found no other donors, he paid the required five thousand francs. On another occasion, riding in the Paris Metro with the bishop, she voiced her discouragement about problems she was then facing. At that exact moment the Metro exited a tunnel and was bathed in the light of day. "You see," said Metropolitan Evlogy, "it is the answer to your question."

The house was completely unfurnished. The first night she wrapped herself in blankets and slept on the floor beneath the icon of the Protection of the Mother of God. Donated furniture began arriving, and also guests, mainly young Russian women without jobs. To make room for others, Mother Maria gave up her own room and instead slept on a narrow iron bedstead in the basement by the boiler. A room upstairs became a chapel, its icon screen painted by Mother Maria, while the dining room doubled as a hall for lectures and dialogues.

In time the house proved too small. Two years later a new location was found — a derelict house of three stories at 77 rue de Lourmel in the fifteenth *arrondissement,* an area where many impoverished Russian refugees had settled. While at the former address she could feed only twenty-five, here she could feed a hundred. The house had the additional advantage of having stables in back, which were now made into a small church. Again the decoration was chiefly her own work, many of its icons made by embroidery, an art in which Mother Maria was skilled. She thought of the new property as a modern Noah's Ark able to withstand the stormy waves the world was hurling its way. Here her guests could regain their breath "until the time comes to stand on their two feet again." Her credo was: "Each person is the very icon of God incarnate in the world." With this recognition came the need "to accept this awesome revelation of God unconditionally, to venerate the image of God" in her brothers and sisters.

As the work evolved she rented other buildings, one for families in need and another for single men. A rural property became a sanatorium. By 1937, there were several dozen women guests at 77 rue de Lourmel. Up to 120 dinners were served each day, normally soup plus a main course that included meat plus plenty of bread supplied gratis by a sympathetic baker.

Mother Maria's day typically began with a journey to Les Halles to beg food or buy cheaply whatever was not donated. The cigarette-smoking beggar nun became well known among the stalls. She would later return with a sack of bones, fish, and overripe fruit and vegetables.

On rue de Lourmel she had a room beneath the stairs next to the kitchen. Here on one occasion a visitor found her collapsed in an armchair in a state of exhaustion. "I can't go on like this," she said. "I can't take anything in. I'm tired, I'm really tired. There have been about forty people here today, each with his own sorrow and needs. I can't chase them away!"

She would sometimes recall the Russian story of the ruble that could never be spent. Each time it was used, the change given back proved to equal a ruble. It was exactly this way with love, she said: No matter how much love you give, you never have less. In fact you discover you have more — one ruble becomes two, two becomes ten.

She would also relate a legend concerning two fourth-century saints, Nicholas of Myra and John Cassian, who returned to earth to see how things were going. They came upon a peasant, his cart mired in the mud, who begged their help. John Cassian regretfully declined, explaining that he was soon due back in heaven and therefore must keep his robes spotless. Meanwhile Nicholas was already up to his hips in the mud, freeing the cart. When the Ruler of All discovered why Nicholas was caked in mud and John Cassian immaculate, it was decided that Nicholas's feast day would henceforth be celebrated twice each year — May 9 and December 6 — while John Cassian's would occur only once every four years, on February 29.

Mother Maria felt sustained by the opening verses of the Sermon on the Mount: "Not only do we know the Beatitudes, but at this hour, this very minute, surrounded though we are by a dismal and despairing world, we already savor the blessedness they promise."

It was no virtue of her own that could account for her activities, she insisted. "There is no hardship in it, since all the relief comes my way. God having given me a compassionate nature, how else could I live?"

Volunteers offered assistance, and in 1937 another nun came to help: Mother Evdokia Meshcherakova. Later Mother Blandina Obolenskaya entered the community. There was also Father Lev Gillet, thanks to whom the liturgy was celebrated frequently. Father Lev lived in an outbuilding near the stable until his departure to London in 1938.

Yet life in community was not easy. Conflicting views about the relative importance of liturgical life were at times a source of tension. Mother Maria was the one most often absent from services or the one who would withdraw early, or arrive late, because of the pressing needs of hospitality. "Piety, piety," she wrote in her journal, "but where is the love that moves mountains?"

Mother Evdokia, who had begun her monastic life in a more traditional context, was not as experimental by temperament as Mother Maria. As the community had no abbess, there was no one to arbitrate between the two. For Mother Evdokia, though always in awe of Mother Maria's endurance and prophetic passion, the house at rue de Lourmel was too much an "ecclesiastical Bohemia." Mother Maria's view was that "the liturgy must be translated into life. It is why Christ came into the world and why he gave us our liturgy." (In 1938 Mother Evdokia and Mother Blandina departed to establish a more traditional monastery at Moisenay-le-Grand.)

Mother Maria clung to her experiment. "In the past religious freedom was trampled down by forces external to Christianity," she wrote. "In Russia we can say that any regime whatsoever will build concentration camps as its response to religious freedom."

She considered exile in the West a heaven-sent opportunity to renew the Church in ways that would have met with repression in her mother country.

What obligations follow from the gift of freedom which [in our exile] we have been granted? We are beyond the reach of persecution. We can write, speak, work, open schools.... At the same time, we have been liberated from age-old traditions. We have no enormous cathedrals, [jewel-]encrusted Gospel books, no monastery walls. We have lost our environment. Is this an accident? Is this some chance misfortune?...In the context of spiritual life, there is no chance, nor are there fortunate or unfortunate epochs. Rather there are signs which we must understand and paths which we must follow. Our calling is a great one, since we are called to freedom.

For her, exile was an opportunity "to liberate the real and authentic" from layers of decoration and dust in which Christ had become hidden. It was similar to the opportunity given to the first Christians. Of paramount importance, "We must not allow Christ to be overshadowed by any regulations, any customs, any traditions, any aesthetic considerations, or even any piety."

Mother Maria's difficulties at times made her feel a terrifying loneliness. "I get very depressed," she admitted. "I could desist, if only I could be convinced that I stand for a truth that is relative."

She was sustained chiefly by those she served — themselves beaten down, people in despair, cripples, alcoholics, the sick, survivors of many tragedies. But not all responded to trust with trust. Theft was not uncommon. On one occasion a guest stole twenty-five francs. Everyone guessed who the culprit was, a drug addict, but Mother Maria refused to accuse her. Instead she announced at the dinner table that the money had not been stolen, only misplaced, and she had found it. "You see how dangerous it is to make accusations," she commented. The girl who stole the money burst into tears.

"It is not enough to give," Mother Maria might say. "We must have a heart that gives." If mistakes were made, if people betrayed a trust, the cure was not to limit giving. "The only ones who make no mistakes," she said, "are those who do nothing."

Mother Maria and her collaborators would not simply open the door when those in need knocked, but would actively seek out the homeless. One place to find them was an all-night café at Les Halles, where those with nowhere else to go could sit as long as they liked for the price of a glass of wine. Children were also cared for. A part-time school was opened at several locations.

Fortunately for the community, their prudent business manager, Fedor Pianov, formerly general secretary of the Russian SCM, at times intervened in cases where trusted persons were systematically violating the confidence placed in them, as sometimes happened.

Turning her attention toward Russian refugees who had been classified insane, Mother Maria began a series of visits to mental hospitals. In each hospital 5 to 10 percent of the Russian patients turned out to be sane and, thanks to her intervention, were released. Language barriers and cultural misunderstandings had kept them in the asylum.

An inquiry into the needs of impoverished Russians suffering from tuberculosis resulted in the opening in 1935 of a sanatorium in Noisy-le-Grand. Its church was a former henhouse. Her efforts bore the unexpected additional fruit of other French TB sanitaria opening their doors to Russian refugees. The house at Noisy, no longer having to serve its original function, then became a rest home. It was here that Mother Maria's mother, Sophia, ended her days in 1962. She was a century old.

Another landmark was the foundation in September 1935 of a group christened Orthodox Action, a name proposed by her friend, the philosopher Nicholas Berdyaev. In addition to Mother Maria and Berdyaev, the co-founders included the theologian Father Sergei Bulgakov, the historian George Fedotov, the literary scholar Constantine Mochulsky, and her long-time co-worker Fedor Pianov. Metropolitan Evlogy was honorary president. Mother Maria was chairman. With financial support coming not only from supporters within France but from other parts of Europe as well as America, a wider range of projects and centers were made possible: hostels, rest homes, schools, camps, hospital work, help to the unemployed, assistance to the elderly, and publication of books and pamphlets.

Mother Maria's driving concern throughout the expansion of work was that it should never lose either its personal or communal character:

We should make every effort to ensure that each of our initiatives is the common work of all those who stand in need of it, and not [simply part of] some charitable organization, where some perform charitable actions and are accountable for it to their superiors while others receive the charity, make way for those who are next in line, and disappear from view. We must cultivate a communal organization rather than set up a mechanical organization, Our concept of *sobornost'* [conciliarity] commits us to this. At the same time we are committed to the personal principle in the sense that absolutely no one can become for us a routine cipher, whose role is to swell statistical tables. I would say that we should not give away a single piece of bread unless the recipient means something as a person for us.

She was certain that there was no other path to heaven than participating in God's mercy:

The way to God lies through love of people. At the Last Judgment I shall not be asked whether I was successful in my ascetic exercises, nor how many bows and prostrations I made. Instead I shall be asked, Did I feed the hungry, clothe the naked, visit the sick and the prisoners. That is all I shall be asked. About every poor, hungry and imprisoned person the Savior says "I": "I was hungry, and thirsty, I was sick and in prison." To think that he puts an equal sign between himself and anyone in need. . . . I always knew it, but now it has somehow penetrated to my sinews. It fills me with awe.

Russians have not been last among those enamored with theories, but for Mother Maria, theory always had to take second place. "We have not gathered together for the theoretical study of social problems in the spirit of Orthodoxy," she wrote in 1939, but "to link our social thought as closely as possible with life and work. More precisely, we proceed from our work and seek the fullest possible theological interpretation of it."

Yet time was also given to abstract inquiry. Sunday afternoons were normally a time for lectures and discussions at rue de Lourmel. Berdyaev, Bulgakov, and Fedotov were frequent speakers. In addition there were courses set up during the week, including sessions of the Religious-Philosophical Academy, which Berdyaev had founded.

While many valued what she and her co-workers were doing, there were others who were scandalized by the shabby nun who was so uncompromising with regard to the duty of hospitality that she might leave a church service to answer the doorbell. "For church circles we are too far to the left," Mother Maria noted, "while for the left we are too church-minded." Those on the left also saw no point in efforts to relieve individual cases of suffering, still less in time given to prayer. One must rather devote all one's efforts to bringing about radical social change. There were also supportive friends, Berdyaev among them, who had little understanding of her monastic vocation, though for Mother Maria this remained at the core of her identity. "Thanks to my being clothed as a nun," she commented, "many things are simpler and within my reach."

In October 1939, Metropolitan Evlogy sent a new priest to rue de Lourmel: Father Dimitri Klepinin, then thirty-five years old. He was a spiritual child of Father Sergei Bulgakov, who had also been one of his teachers. A man of few words and great modesty, Father Dimitri proved to be a real partner for Mother Maria.

The last phase of Mother Maria's life was a series of responses to World War II and Germany's occupation of France. It would have been possible for her to leave Paris when the Germans were advancing toward the city, or even to leave the country to go to America. Her decision was not to budge. "If the Germans take Paris, I shall stay here with my old women. Where else could I send them?"

She had no illusions about the Nazi threat. It represented a "new paganism" bringing in its wake disasters, upheavals, persecutions, and wars. It was evil unveiled, the "contaminator of all springs and wells." The so-called "master race" was "led by a madman who needs a straightjacket and should be placed in a cork-lined room so that his bestial wailing will not disturb the world at large." "We are entering eschatological times," she wrote. "Do you not feel that the end is already near?"

Death seemed to rule the world. "Right now, at this moment, I know that hundreds of people are face to face with what is most serious, with Seriousness itself — with death; I know that thousands and thousands of people are waiting their turn," she wrote at Easter in 1940. "I know that mothers are watching for the mailman and tremble when a letter comes a day late." But she saw one gain in all this: "Everything is clearly in its place. Everyone must make a choice. There is nothing disguised or hypocritical in the enemy's approach."

Paris fell on June 14. France capitulated a week later. With defeat came greater poverty and hunger for many people. Local authorities in Paris declared the house at rue de Lourmel an official food distribution point — Cantine Municipale No. 9. Here volunteers sold at cost whatever food Mother Maria had bought that morning at Les Halles.

Paris was now a great prison. "There is the dry clatter of iron, steel, and brass," wrote Mother Maria. "Order is all." Russian refugees were among the particular targets of the occupiers. In June 1941, a thousand were arrested, including several close friends and collaborators of Mother Maria and Father Dimitri. An aid project for prisoners and their dependents was soon launched by Mother Maria.

Early in 1942, their registration now under way, Jews began to knock on the door at rue de Lourmel asking Father Dimitri if he would issue baptismal certificates to them. The answer was always yes. The names of those "baptized" were also duly recorded in his parish register in case there was any cross-checking by the police or Gestapo, as indeed did happen. Father Dimitri was convinced that in such a situation Christ would do the same.

When the Nazis issued special identity cards for those of Russian origin living in France, with Jews being specially identified, Mother Maria and Father Dimitri refused to comply, though they were warned that those who failed to register would be regarded as citizens of the USSR — enemy aliens — and punished accordingly.

In March 1942, the order came from Berlin that the yellow star must be worn by Jews in all the occupied countries. The order came into force in France in June. There were, of course, Christians who said that the law being imposed had nothing to do with Christians and that therefore this was not a Christian problem. "There is no such thing as a Christian problem," Mother Maria replied. "Don't you realize that the battle is being waged against Christianity? If we were true Christians we would all wear the Star. The age of confessors has arrived."

She wrote a poem reflecting on the symbol Jews were required to wear:

> Two triangles, a star,
> The shield of King David, our forefather.
> This is election, not offense.
> The great path and not an evil.
>
> Once more is a term fulfilled,
> Once more roars the trumpet of the end;
> And the fate of a great people
> Once more is by the prophet proclaimed.
> Thou art persecuted again, O Israel,
> But what can human malice mean to thee,
> who have heard the thunder from Sinai?[4]

In July Jews were forbidden access to nearly all public places. Shopping by Jews was restricted to one hour per day. A week later, there was a mass arrest of Jews — 12,884, of whom 6,900 (two-thirds of them children) were brought to the Vélodrome d'Hiver sports stadium just a kilometer from rue de Lourmel. Held there for five days, the captives in the stadium received water only from a single hydrant, while ten latrines were supposed to serve them all. From there the captives were to be sent via Drancy to Auschwitz.

Mother Maria had often thought her monastic robe a godsend in aiding her work. Now it opened the way for her to enter the stadium. Here she worked for three days trying to comfort the children and their parents, distributing what food she could bring in, even managing to rescue a number of children by enlisting the aid of garbage collectors and smuggling them out in trash bins.

The house at rue de Lourmel was bursting with people, many of them Jews. "It is amazing," Mother Maria remarked, "that the Germans haven't pounced on us yet." In the same period, she said if anyone came looking for Jews, she would show them an icon of the Mother of God.

Father Dimitri, Mother Maria, and their co-workers set up routes of escape, from Lourmel to Noisy-le-Grand and from there to other, safer destinations in the unoccupied south. It was complex and dangerous work. Forged documents had to be obtained. An escaped Russian prisoner of war was also among those assisted, working for a time in the Lourmel kitchen. In turn, a local resistance group helped secure provisions for those Mother Maria's community was struggling to feed.

On February 8, 1943, while Mother Maria was traveling, Nazi security police entered the house on rue de Lourmel and found a letter in her son Yura's pocket, in which Father Dimitri was asked to provide a Jew with a false baptismal document. Yura, now actively a part of his mother's work, was taken to the office of Orthodox Action, soon after followed by his distraught grandmother, Sophia Pilenko. The interrogator, Hans Hoffman, a Gestapo officer who spoke Russian, ordered her to bring Father Dimitri. Once the priest was there, Hoffman said, they would let Yura go. His grandmother was allowed to embrace Yura and give him a blessing, making the sign of the cross on his body. It was the last time she saw him in this world.

The following morning Father Dimitri served the liturgy at rue de Lourmel in a side chapel dedicated to St. Philip, a bishop who had paid with his life for protesting the crimes of Tsar Ivan the Terrible. Fortified by communion he set off for the Gestapo office on rue des Saussies. Interrogated for four hours, he made no attempt to hide his beliefs. A fragment of their exchange survives:

Hoffman: If we release you, will you give your word never again to aid Jews?

Klepinin: I can say no such thing. I am a Christian and must act as I must. (Hoffman struck Klepinin across the face.)

Hoffman: Jew lover! How dare you talk of helping those swine as being a Christian duty!

(Klepinin, recovering his balance, held up the cross from his cassock.)

Klepinin: Do you know *this* Jew?

(For this, Father Dimitri was knocked to the floor.)

"Your priest did himself in," Hoffman said afterward to Sophia Pilenko. "He insists that if he were to be freed, he would act exactly as before."

The next day, February 10, Mother Maria was back in Paris and was also arrested by Hoffman, who brought her back to rue de Lourmel while he searched her room. Several others were called for questioning and then held by the Gestapo, including a visitor to the home of Father Dimitri. His wife, Tamara, sensing the danger she was in and aware that she was powerless to free her husband, left Paris with their two young children, one four, the other six months old. The three survived.

Arrested a week later at rue de Lourmel, Mother Maria saw her mother for the last time. "We embraced," her mother recalled. "I blessed her. We had lived all our life together, in friendship, hardly ever apart. She bade me farewell and said, as she always did at the most difficult moments, 'Mother, be strong.'"

Mother Maria was confined with thirty-four other women at the Gestapo headquarters in Paris. Her son Yura, Father Dimitri, and their co-worker of many years, Feodor Pianov, were being held in the same building. Pianov later recalled the scene of Father Dimitri in his torn cassock being taunted as a Jew. One of the SS began to prod and beat him while Yura stood nearby weeping. Father Dimitri "began to console him, saying the Christ withstood greater mockery than this."

In April the prisoners were transferred to Compiègne, and here Mother Maria was blessed with a final meeting with Yura, who crawled through a window in order to see her. In a letter Yura sent to the community at rue de Lourmel, he said his mother "was in a remarkable state of mind and told me...that I must trust in her ability to bear things and in general not to worry about her. Every day [Father Dimitri and I] remember her at the *proskomidia*....[5] We celebrate the Eucharist and receive communion each day." He told his mother that his favorite prayer had become the Jesus Prayer — "Lord Jesus Christ, Son of God, have mercy on me a sinner" — and that it provided a way for him to stay close to her no matter what happened. Hours after their meeting, Mother Maria was transported to Germany.

"Thanks to our daily Eucharist," another letter from Yura reported, "our life here is quite transformed and to tell the honest truth, I have nothing to complain of. We live in brotherly love. Dima [Father Dimitri] and I speak to each other as tu [the intimate form of 'you'] and he is preparing me for the priesthood. God's will needs to be understood. After all, this attracted me all my life and in the end it was the only thing I was interested in, though my interest was stifled by Parisian life and the illusion that there might be 'something better' — as if there could be anything better."

In a letter Father Dimitri sent to his wife, he reported that their church was "a very good one." It was a barracks room transformed, as many other unlikely structures had been in the past. They even managed to make an icon screen and reading stand.

For a year the three men remained together at Compiègne. "Without exaggeration," Pianov wrote after being liberated in 1945, "I can say that the year spent with [Father Dimitri] was a godsend. I do not regret that year.... From my experience with him, I learned to understand what enormous spiritual, psychological, and moral support one man can give to others as a friend, companion, and confessor."

On December 16, Yura and Father Dimitri were deported to Buchenwald concentration camp in Germany, followed several weeks later by Pianov. In January 1944, Father Dimitri and Yura — now in striped prison uniforms and with shaved heads — were sent to another camp, Dora, forty kilometers away, where parts for V-1 and V-2 rockets were being manufactured in underground factories. Within ten days of arrival, Yura contracted furunculosis, a condition in which large areas of the skin are covered in boils. On February 6, he was "dispatched for treatment" — a euphemism for sentenced to death. Four days later Father Dimitri, lying on a dirt floor, died of pneumonia. His body was disposed of in the Buchenwald crematorium.

A final letter from Yura, written at Compiègne, was discovered in a suitcase of his possessions returned from the camp to rue de Lourmel:

> My dears, Dima [Father Dimitri] blesses you, my most beloved ones. I am to go to Germany with Dima, Father Andrei [who also died in a concentration camp], and Anatoly [Vishkovsky]. I am absolutely calm, even somewhat proud to share mama's fate. I promise you I will bear everything with dignity. Whatever happens, sooner or later we shall all be together. I can say in all honesty that I am not afraid of anything any longer.... I ask anyone whom I have hurt in any way to forgive me. Christ be with you!

Mother Maria, prisoner 19263, was sent in a sealed cattle truck from Compiègne to the Ravensbrück camp in Germany, where she endured for two years, an achievement in part explained by her long experience of ascetic life. She was assigned to Block 27 in the large camp's southwest corner. Not far away was Block 31, full of Russian prisoners, many of whom she managed to befriend.

Because she was unable to correspond with friends, little testimony in her own words has come down to us, but prisoners who survived the war remembered her. One of them, Solange Périchon, recalled:

She was never downcast, never. She never complained.... She was full of good cheer, really good cheer. We had roll calls which lasted a great deal of time. We were wakened at three in the morning, and we had to stand out in the open in the middle of winter until the barracks [population] was counted. She took all this calmly and she would say, "Well, that's that. Yet another day completed. And tomorrow it will be the same all over again. But one fine day the time will come for all of this to end." She was on good terms with everyone. Anyone in the block, no matter who it was, knew her on equal terms. She was the kind of person who made no distinction between people [whether they] held extremely progressive political views [or had] religious beliefs radically different from her own. She allowed nothing of secondary importance to impede her contact with people.

Another prisoner, Rosane Lascroux, recalled:

She exercised an enormous influence on us all. No matter what our nationality, age, political convictions — this had no significance whatever. Mother Maria was adored by all. The younger prisoners gained particularly from her concern. She took us under her wing. We were cut off from our families, and somehow she provided us with a family.

In a memoir, Jacqueline Péry stressed the importance of the talks Mother Maria gave and the discussion groups she led:

She used to organize real discussion circles ... and I had the good fortune to participate in them. Here was an oasis at the end of the day. She would tell us about her social work, about how she conceived the reconciliation of the Orthodox and Catholic Churches. We would question her about the history of Russia, about its future, about Communism, about her frequent contacts with young women from the Soviet army with whom she liked to surround herself. These discussions, whatever their subject matter, provided an escape from the hell in which we lived. They allowed us to restore our depleted morale, they rekindled in us the flame of thought, which barely flickered beneath the heavy burden of horror.

Often, Péry wrote, she would recite passages from the New Testament: "Together we would provide a commentary on the texts and then meditate on them. Often we would conclude with Compline.... This period seemed a paradise to us."

Yet, as was recalled by another prisoner, Sophia Nosovich, Mother Maria "never preached but rather discussed religion simply with those who sought it, causing them to understand it and to exercise their minds, not merely their feelings. Whatever and however she could, she would sustain the as yet incompletely extinguished flame of humanity, no matter what form it took."

The same former prisoner wrote that "it was not submissiveness which gave [Mother Maria] strength to bear the suffering, but the integrity and wealth of her interior life."

And all this happened in what Mother Maria described not as a prison but as hell itself, nothing less, a bestial place in which obscenity, contempt, and hatred were normal and where hunger, illness, and death were a daily event. In such a climate, many opted for the numbing of all feeling and withdrawal as a survival strategy while others, in their despair, looked forward only to death.

"I once said to Mother Maria," wrote Sophia Nosovich, "that it was more than a question of my ceasing to feel anything whatsoever. My very thought processes were numbed and had ground to a halt. 'No, no,' Mother Maria responded, 'whatever you do, continue to think. In the conflict with doubt, cast your thought wider and deeper. Let it transcend the conditions and the limitations of this earth.'"

One prisoner even recalled how Mother Maria had used the ever-smoking chimneys of the crematoria as a metaphor of hope rather than being seen as the only exit point from the camp. "But it is only here, immediately above the chimneys, that the billows of smoke are oppressive," Mother Maria said. "When they rise higher, they turn into light clouds before being dispersed in limitless space. In the same way, our souls, once they have torn themselves away from this sinful earth, move by means of an effortless unearthly flight into eternity, where there is life full of joy."

Anticipating that her own exit point from the camp might be via the crematoria chimneys, she asked a fellow prisoner whom she hoped would survive to memorize a message to be given at last to Father Sergei Bulgakov, Metropolitan Evlogy, and her mother: "My state at present is such that I completely accept suffering in the knowledge that this is how things ought to be for me, and if I am to die, I see this as a blessing from on high."

In a postcard she was allowed to send friends in Paris in the fall of 1944, she said she remained strong and healthy but had "altogether become an old woman."

Her work in the camp varied. There was a period when she was part of a team of women dragging a heavy iron roller about the roads and pathways of the camp for twelve hours a day. In another period she worked in a knitwear workshop.

Her legs began to give way. At roll call another prisoner, Inna Webster, would act as her crutches. As her health declined, friends no longer allowed her to give away portions of her own food, as she had done in the past to help keep others alive.

Friends who survived recalled that Mother Maria wrote two poems while at Ravensbrück, but sadly neither survive. However a kerchief she embroidered for Rosane Lascroux, made with a needle and thread stolen from the tailoring workshop, at last came out of the camp intact. In the style of the medieval Bayeux Tapestry, it was a depiction of the Allies' Normandy Landing in June 1944. Her final embroidered icon, purchased with the price of her precious bread ration, was of the Mother of God holding the infant Jesus, her child already marked with the wounds of the cross.

With the Red Army approaching from the east, the concentration camp administrators further reduced food rations while greatly increasing the population of each block from eight hundred to twenty-five hundred. "People slept three to a bunk," a survivor recalls. "Lice devoured us. Typhus and dysentery became a common scourge and decimated our ranks."

By March 1945, Mother Maria's condition was critical. She had to lie down between roll calls and hardly spoke. Her face, as Jacqueline Péry recalled, "revealed intense inner suffering. Already it bore the marks of death. Nevertheless Mother Maria made no complaint. She kept her eyes closed and seemed to be in a state of continual prayer. This was, I think, her Garden of Gethsemane."

In November–December 1944, she accepted a pink card that was freely issued to any prisoner who wished to be excused from labor because of age or ill health. In January all who had received such cards were rounded up and transferred to what was called the Jugendlager — the "youth camp" — where the camp authorities said each person would have her own bed and abundant food. Mother Maria's transfer was on January 31. Here the food ration was further reduced and the hours spent standing for roll calls increased. Though it was mid-winter, blankets, coats, and jackets were confiscated, and then even shoes and stockings. The death rate was at least fifty per day. Next all medical supplies were withdrawn. Those who still persisted in surviving now faced death by shootings and gas, the latter made possible by the construction of a gas chamber in March 1945. In this 150 were executed per day.

It is astonishing that Mother Maria lasted five weeks in the "youth camp," and was finally sent back to the main camp on March 3. Though emaciated and infested with lice, with her eyes festering, she began to think she might actually live to return to Paris, or even go back to Russia.

That same month the camp commander received an order from Reichsführer Himmler that anyone who could no longer walk should be killed. While such orders had been anticipated and many already killed, the decree accelerated the process. With the help of Inna Webster and others to lean on, Mother Maria managed to continue standing at roll calls, but this became far more difficult when groups of prisoners were ordered into ranks of five for purposes of selecting those to be killed that day. Within her block, Mother Maria was sometimes hidden in a small space between roof and ceiling in expectation of raids in which additional "selections" were made.

The last phase of her life began on the 30th of March, Good Friday as it happened. The shellfire of the approaching Red Army could be heard in the distance.

Accounts are at odds about what happened. According to one, she was simply one of the many selected for death that day. According to another, she took the place of another prisoner who had been chosen. Her friend Jacqueline Péry wrote afterward: "It is very possible that [Mother Maria] took the place of a frantic companion. It would have been entirely in keeping with her generous life. In any case she offered herself consciously to the holocaust...thus assisting each one of us to accept the cross.... She radiated the peace of God and communicated it to us."

Although perishing in the gas chamber, she did not perish in the Church's memory. Survivors of the war who had known her would again and again draw attention to the ideas, insights, and activities of the maverick nun who had spent so many years coming to the aid of people in desperate straits. Soon after the end of World War II, essays and books about her began appearing, in French and Russian. A Russian film, *Mother Maria*, was made in 1982. There have been two biographies in English and little by little the translation and publication in English of her most notable essays.[6]

Controversial in life, Mother Maria remains a subject of contention to this day, a fact which may explain the slowness of the Orthodox Church in adding her to the calendar of saints. While clearly she lived a life of heroic virtue and is among the martyrs of the twentieth century, her verbal assaults on nationalistic and tradition-bound forms of religious life still raise the blood pressure of many Orthodox Christians. Mother Maria remains an indictment of any form of Christianity that seeks Christ chiefly inside church buildings.

Especially in America, the life of Mother Maria will remind many people of Dorothy Day, another social radical who, following her conversion, devoted herself to hospitality and protest. Both were born in the same decade. While Mother Maria's life was cut short by martyrdom, other parallels between the two are numerous, not least in what they had to say on the printed page.

Many paragraphs in the writing of Mother Maria could have been written by Dorothy Day, and vice versa. Though Dorothy Day was a devoted Catholic and Mother Maria was similarly committed to the Orthodox Church, both were ecumenically attuned in a time when such attitudes were rare.

My hope for this small book is that it will not only introduce a remarkable Christian to readers who are hearing of her for the first time, but help pave the way toward renewed experiments in religious life such as those Mother Maria began in France.

1

The Second Gospel
Commandment

Undoubtedly Mother Maria's most important insight was the realization that our love of God cannot be separated from our love for the neighbor. While this reality might seem obvious, she reveals how both traditional religiosity and the machinations of our consciousness subtly tend to divide these two loves. Mother Maria grounds her argument in Scripture, the spirit of liturgical prayer, the wisdom of the Church Fathers, the principles of Orthodox philosophy, and the very "triune" nature of the human being: body, soul, and spirit. But ultimately, this piece reflects her own distinctive vision of the relationship between religious life and social action, a theme that winds its way through all of her writings.

There exists in the Christian world a constant tendency, in moments of various historical catastrophes, to preach with great intensity an immersion in oneself, a withdrawal from life, a standing of the solitary human soul before God.

It appears to me that now, too, this tendency is beginning to show itself very strongly, producing a strange picture of the world: on one side all the diverse forces of evil, united and affirming the power of the collective, of the masses, and the worthlessness and insignificance of each separate human soul; and on the other side — dispersed and disunited Christian souls, affirming themselves in this dispersion and disunity, for whom the world becomes a sort of evil phantom, and the only reality is God and my solitary soul trembling before Him.

It seems to me that this state of mind is definitely a temptation, is definitely as terrible for each person as it is for the destiny of the Church of Christ, and I would like to rise against it with all my strength and call people to each other, to stand together before God, to suffer sorrows together, to resist temptations together. And I can find an enormous number of indisputable reasons for this call, in all areas of Christian life.

I will begin with what is perceived as most personal and intimate, the area which everyone knows to be precisely the one where the soul stands alone before God — with Orthodox prayers and, to limit myself still further, not with the prayers of the Church, uttered during church services, where their non-personal character goes without saying, but precisely with the personal prayers, known to everyone, which are said at home behind closed doors. I am thinking of the usual order of morning and evening prayers, which can be found in any prayer book and to which we have been accustomed since childhood. The important thing for me is to establish that an absolute majority of them are addressed to God from *us* and not from *me*. I want to look at them from that point of view.

They begin like this: "Glory to Thee, *our* God, glory to Thee." The prayer "O Heavenly King" ends with the words: "Come and abide in *us,* cleanse *us* from every impurity, and save *our* souls, O Good One." The Trisagion[7] ends: "have mercy on *us.*" Then: "Lord, cleanse *us* from *our* sins, Master, pardon *our* transgressions, Holy One, visit *us* and heal us of *our* infirmities for Thy name's sake." Further on comes the Lord's Prayer, beginning with the address: "*Our* Father.... Give *us* this day *our* daily bread; and forgive *us* our debts, as *we* forgive *our* debtors. And lead *us* not into temptation, but deliver *us* from the evil one."

In the morning prayers, the plural is used as definitely and as clearly. "*We* fall down before Thee, *we* sing unto Thee ... have mercy on *us.* ... O come, let *us* worship God, *our* King ... receive *our* prayer...cleanse *us* and heal *us*...that *we* may be found ready...for Thou hast borne the savior of *our* souls...."

Further on come prayers for the living and the departed, that is, for others, not for oneself. Exactly the same thing is repeated in the evening prayers. Thus what is most personal, what is most intimate in an Orthodox person's life, is thoroughly pervaded by this sense of being united with everyone, the sense of the principle of *sobornost'*,[8] characteristic of the Orthodox Church. This is a fact of great significance; this forces us to reflect.

If this is so in a person's private prayer, there is no need to speak of prayer in the church. A priest cannot even celebrate the liturgy if he is alone; for that he must have at least one person who symbolizes the people. And the eucharistic mystery itself is precisely the common work of the Church, accomplished on behalf of all and for all.

It would be an unseemly protestantizing on the part of Orthodox people if they forgot these central and most characteristic particularities of their Orthodox truth. In the Orthodox Church man is not alone and his path to salvation is not solitary; he is a member of the Body of Christ, he shares the fate of his brothers in Christ, he is justified by the righteous and bears responsibility for the sins of the sinners. The Orthodox Church is not a solitary standing before God, but *sobornost'*, which binds everyone with the bonds of Christ's love and the love for one another. And that is not something invented by theologians and philosophers, but a precise teaching of the Gospel, brought to life through the centuries of existence of the Church's body. Khomiakov, Dostoevsky, and Soloviev,[9] who did much to explain these truths to broad segments of Russian educated society, were able to confirm it by references to the Word of God, to precise teachings from the Savior. The Orthodox man only fulfills the precepts of his faith when he takes them as a certain bi-une commandment of love for God and love for one's neighbor.

There occur, of course, whole epochs of deviation from the right attitude toward this bi-unity. And it is especially characteristic of periods of catastrophe and general instability, when man in his pusillanimity tries to hide, to take cover, and not deal with anyone who belongs to this tottering world. It seems to him that if he remembers God alone, and stands before Him in his soul in order to save it, he will thereby be delivered from all calamity and remain clean in a time of universal defilement. Such a man should tirelessly repeat to himself the words of St. John the Theologian about hypocrites who say they love God without loving man [1 Jn 4:20]. How can they love God, whom they do not see, and hate their brother, who is near them? For the fulfillment of love for one's neighbor, Christ demanded that we lay down our soul for our friends. Here there is no sense in paraphrasing this demand and saying that it has to do not with the soul but with life, because when the apostle Paul says, about the fulfilling of Christ's demand, that he could wish he were separated from Christ, so long as he could see his brothers saved [Rom 9:3] — it is clear that he is speaking of the state of his soul, and not only his life.

Equally irrefutable is Christ's teaching about how we should deal with our neighbor, in His words about the Last Judgment [Mt 25:31–45], when man will be asked not how he saved his soul by solitary endeavor but precisely how he dealt with his neighbor, whether he visited him in prison, whether he fed him when he was hungry, comforted him — in short, whether he loved his fellow man, whether this love stood before him as an immutable commandment of Christ. And here we cannot excuse ourselves from active love, from the selfless giving of our soul for our friends.

But even if we set aside the separate and particular Gospel teachings in this regard and turn to the whole activity of Christ on earth, it is here that we find the highest degree of the laying down of one's soul for others, the highest measure of sacrificial love and self-giving that mankind has known. "For God so loved the world that He gave His only-begotten Son" [Jn 3:16], calling us, too, to the same love. There is not and there cannot be any following in the steps of Christ without taking upon ourselves a certain share, small as it may be, of participation in this sacrificial deed of love. Anyone who loves the world, anyone who lays down his soul for others, anyone who is ready, at the price of

being separated from Christ, to gain salvation for his brothers —
is a disciple and follower of Christ. And inversely, anyone who
abides in the temptation of self-salvation alone, anyone who does
not take upon himself the responsibility for the pain and sin of
the world, anyone who follows the path of "egoism," be it even
"holy" egoism, simply does not hear what Christ says, and does
not see what His sacrifice on Golgotha was offered for.

Here it is important to stress once more that quite often various exercises in external virtue — feeding vagabonds, sheltering
beggars, and so on — are also accepted, as it were, by those who
follow the path of self-salvation. But they are accepted as ascetic
exercises useful for the soul. Of course, this is not the love that
the Gospel teaches us, and it was not for this kind of love that
Christ was crucified. His love, given to us in inheritance, is true
sacrificial love, the giving of the soul not in order to receive it
back with interest, so to speak, not as an act in its own name,
but as an act in the name of a neighbor, and only in his name,
our love for whom reveals to us the image of God in him. Here
we cannot reason like this: Christ gave us the firm and true teaching that we meet Him in every poor and unhappy man. Let us
take that into consideration and give this poor and unhappy man
our love, because he only seems poor and unhappy to us, but in
fact he is the King of Heaven, and with Him our gifts will not
go for nothing, but will return to us a hundredfold. No, the poor
and unhappy man is indeed poor and unhappy, and in him Christ
is indeed present in a humiliated way, and we receive him in the
name of the love of Christ, not because we will be rewarded, but
because we are aflame with this sacrificial love of Christ and in it
we are united with Him, with His suffering on the Cross, and we
suffer not for the sake of our purification and salvation, but for
the sake of this poor and unhappy man whose suffering is alle-
viated by ours. One cannot love sacrificially in one's own name,
but only in the name of Christ, in the name of the image of God
that is revealed to us in man.

All these Gospel teachings we have referred to may be taken
as random or tendentious. We know that heretics and sectarians
support their arguments with Gospel texts. It seems we need to

support ourselves with something else, to show that such an interpretation existed throughout the centuries of the history of the
Orthodox Church, for instance, in the *Philokalia*.[10] That is right,
of course, though it calls for certain reservations. The first thing
we need to remember is that the *Philokalia* is not Holy Scripture,
a divinely inspired revelation, but the writings of saints, who are
people after all. The second thing is that in the *Philokalia* the
writings of the authors are not printed in their entirety, but only
as a selection, only, for the most part, in those fragments which
concern instructions for the ascetic endeavor of an individual person. Therefore there is little mention of themes dealing with what
presently concerns us.

Thus, for instance, we may note that in the first volume of
the *Philokalia*, material about the attitude toward one's neighbor
takes up only two pages out of six hundred, and in the second
volume, only three out of seven hundred and fifty. The proportion
is quite different from that in the Gospels or the Epistles. And we
cannot say that it all refers to the direct question of fulfilling the
commandment of the love of God — three-quarters of the remaining material in the *Philokalia* speak mainly about fighting against
gluttony, lasciviousness, and other passions.... But there are texts
of a different sort, which follow wholly from Christ's teaching
about laying down one's soul for one's neighbor. Considering the
generally small number of texts about one's neighbor, these are
still less numerous than the previous kind.

Macarius the Great (ca. 300–390) says:

> Those to whom it has been granted to become children of
> God and to be born from on high of the Holy Spirit...
> sometimes weep and lament, as it were, over the human
> race and, praying for the whole of Adam, shed tears and cry,
> burning with spiritual love for mankind. Sometimes their
> spirit flares up with such joy and love that, if it were pos-
> sible, they would take every man into their heart, wicked
> or good, without distinction. Sometimes, in the humility of
> their spirit, they so abase themselves before each man that
> they consider themselves the least and smallest of all.

In St. John Cassian [ca. 350–435] there is the following state-
ment:

> When someone has no compassion for another's transgres-
> sions, but pronounces a severe judgment on them, it is an
> obvious sign of a soul not yet purified of evil passions.

Particularly remarkable are the thoughts of St. Nilus of Sinai
[fifth century]:

> It is righteous to pray not only for your own purification,
> but for the purification of every man, in imitation of the
> angelic orders.
>
> Blessed is the monk who considers every man as God
> after God. Blessed is the monk who looks upon the accom-
> plishment of the salvation and furtherance of everyone as
> upon his own. Blessed is the monk who considers himself
> the refuse of all. A monk is he who, while withdrawing
> from all, is united with all. A monk is he who considers
> himself as being with everyone and who sees himself in
> everyone.
>
> Prefer nothing to the love of your neighbor, except in
> those cases when because of it the love of God is neglected.

The same spirit breathes in the word of Ephrem the Syrian [ca.
306–373]:

> This is what "Thy will be done on earth as it is in heaven"
> means: when we are united with each other in unenvious-
> ness, simplicity, love, peace, and joy, considering the fur-
> therance of our neighbor as our own gain, and regarding
> his ailments, or failures, or sorrows as our own deficiency,
> as it is said: "Look not every man on his own things, but
> every man also on the things of others" (Phil 2:4). Being
> thus compassionate to each other, especially the strong for
> the weak and the firm for the ailing, we should be able to
> fulfill the law of Christ.
>
> The sign of humility is to satisfy the needs of your
> brother with both hands, in the same way as you would
> receive assistance for yourself.

Let us take care to acquire the eternal blessings promised us. Let us be zealous about it, before it turns dark, before the market closes. Let us make friends of the poor and destitute for our life there. Let us buy oil from them and send them there ahead of us. For it is here that the widows, the orphans, the sick, the lame, the halt, the blind and all the beggars sitting by the church door sell oil for our lamps there.

And, finally, I would like to add to this some texts from St. Isaac the Syrian [seventh century]:

The sign of those who have reached perfection is this: if ten times a day they are given over to be burned for the love of their neighbor, they will not be satisfied with that, as Moses, and the ardent Paul, and the other disciples showed. God gave His Son over to death on the Cross out of love for His creature. And if He had had something more precious, he would have given it to us, in order thereby to gain humankind. Imitating this, all the saints, in striving for perfection, long to be like God in perfect love for their neighbor.

No man dares to say of his love for his neighbor that he succeeds in it in his soul, if he abandons the part that he fulfills bodily, as well as he can, and in conformity with time and place. For only this fulfillment certifies that a man has perfect love in him. And when we are faithful and true in it as far as possible, then the soul is given power, in simple and incomparable notions, to attain to the great region of lofty and divine contemplation.

These words thoroughly justify not only active Christianity, but the possibility of attaining to "lofty and divine contemplation" through the love of one's neighbor — not merely an abstract, but necessarily the most concrete, practical love. Here is the whole key to the mystery of human communion as a religious path.

And two more texts:

If a merciful man is not higher than his truth, then he is not merciful — that is, a truly merciful man not only gives alms of what is his own, but also joyfully suffers wrongs from others and is merciful to them. He who lays down his soul for his brother is merciful, and not he who shows mercy by giving alms.

And the last:

Though you be persecuted, do not persecute. Though you be offended, do not offend. Though you be slandered, do not slander.... Be glad with those who are glad and weep with those who weep, for that is the sign of purity. Be sick with the sick. Shed tears with the sinners. Rejoice with the repentant. Be friends with all men, but in your thought abide alone.

For me these are truly fiery words, and it is not so important that they take up so few pages in the many volumes of the *Philokalia*. The most important thing is that they exist, and by the fact of their existence create a patristic tradition that justifies our search for a path precisely in this direction. Thus we may say boldly that such a tradition exists. Unfortunately, in the area of applying these principles to life, in the area of practical and ascetic behavior toward man, we have much less material than in the area of man's relation to God and to himself. Yet the need to find some precise and correct ways, and not to wander about, guided only by our own sentiments, the need to know the limits of this area of human communion — all this makes itself very strongly felt. In the end, since we have certain basic teachings, perhaps it will not be so difficult to apply them to various areas of human communion, at first only as a sort of schema, an approximate listing of what is involved.

Let us try to find the main landmarks for this schema in the triune makeup of the human being — body, soul, and spirit. In the area of our serving each of these main principles, ascetic demands and teachings emerge of themselves, the fulfillment of which, on the one hand, is unavoidable in order to reach the goal, and, on the other hand, is beyond our strength. It seems right to me to draw a line here between one's attitude toward oneself and one's attitude toward others. The rule of not doing to others what you do not want done to yourself is hardly applicable in asceticism. Asceticism goes much further and sets much stricter demands on oneself than on one's neighbors.

In the area of the relation to one's physical world, asceticism demands two things of us: work and abstinence. Work is not only an unavoidable evil, the curse of Adam; it is also a participation in the work of divine economy; it can be transfigured and sanctified. It is also wrong to reduce work only to working with one's hands, a menial task; it calls for responsibility, inspiration, and love. It should always be work in the fields of the Lord. Work stands at the center of modern ascetic endeavor in the area of man's relation to his physical existence. Abstinence is as unavoidable as work. But its significance is to some degree secondary, because it is needed mainly in order to free one's attention for more valuable things than those from which one abstains. One can introduce a certain unsuitable passion into abstinence — and that is wrong. A person should abstain and at the same time not notice his abstinence.

A person should have a more attentive attitude toward his brother's flesh than toward his own. Christian love teaches us to give our brother not only material but also spiritual gifts. We must give him our last shirt and our last crust of bread. Here personal charity is as necessary and justified as the broadest social work. In this sense there is no doubt that the Christian is called to social work. He is called to organize a better life for the workers, to provide for the old, to build hospitals, care for children, fight against exploitation, injustice, want, lawlessness. In principle the value is completely the same, whether he acts on an individual or a social level; what matters is that his social work be based on love for his neighbor and not have any latent career or material purposes. For the rest it is always justified — from personal aid to working on a national scale, from concrete attention to an individual person to an understanding of abstract systems for the correct organization of social life. The love of man demands one thing from us in this area: ascetic ministry to his material needs, attentive and responsible work, a sober and unsentimental awareness of our strength and of its true usefulness.

The ascetic rules here are simple and perhaps do not leave any particular room for mystical inspiration, often being limited merely to everyday work and responsibility. But there is great strength and great truth in them, based on the words of the Gospel about the Last Judgment, when Christ says to those who stand on His right hand that they visited Him in prison, and in the hospital, fed Him when He was hungry, clothed Him when He was naked. He will say this to those who did it either on an individual or on a social level. Thus, in the dull, laborious, often humdrum ascetic rules concerning our attitude toward the material needs of our neighbor, there already lies the pledge of a possible relation to God, their spirit-bearing nature.

Then comes man's inner world. What should our attitude be toward his inner world? Very often people not only deny it any value, but experience it as something that should be fought against until it is all but totally destroyed. And we see how man, through strenuous efforts, achieves strange results — dryness, indifference, coldness, lovelessness, dispiritedness. These results themselves speak for the fact that something is not right here. For, in the end, man is so made that he cannot destroy his inwardness. He can only pervert, deaden, freeze, ossify it. A right attitude toward his inwardness has all the same criteria. An inwardness that fences man off from the outside world and limits him to the sphere of his own feelings, that concentrates him on following attentively the slightest impulses of his own soul — is the wrong kind of inwardness. An inwardness that allows man to approach the other more closely and with greater attentiveness, that opens to him the inner causes and motives of behavior of another soul, that creates a bridge between man and his neighbor, that teaches him to love his neighbor — is the right kind of inwardness. Inwardness is threatened by two opposite dangers: on the one hand, it is a broad road for passions; on the other hand, through it death comes into the human soul. In order not to give power to passions, man, in the area of his inner life, should not

allow himself any cult of "his own," of the exclusive, even with
what is supposedly most important. To avoid the second danger,
he should not destroy his inwardness, but transform it entirely
into an instrument of love for the other.

And here we pass over to what our attitude should be toward
another person's inner world. An absence of mercenary interest,
of a certain curiosity and relishing of another person's experiences, should be combined in the first place with a strenuous
goodwill, with a sort of genuine tirelessness with regard to another soul. One should be able literally "to put oneself in the
place" of the other person, try to evaluate and experience what
he feels in himself, to be everyone for everyone. Even another
man's passions should be judged, not from outside, but by entering the inner atmosphere of the one who experiences them. We
must have the strength not to define generally what a given man
should or should not do, but to define him from within his own
inner state, to seek to free him from his passions and emotions
not by cutting them off maximally, but by a conscious and profound overcoming, shifting, transfiguring of them. Here, again,
there are two opposite dangers. On the one hand, it is dangerous
to approach a man with the yardstick of all-measuring doctrine
and begin to dissect his living and sick soul; on the other hand, it
is no less dangerous to accept sentimentally the whole of a man as
he is, his soul along with all its sores and growths. The measure
is given by attention, sobriety, and love.

Finally, the area of the spirit demands the greatest effort in
one's attitude toward the other and toward oneself. Of course,
there are a great many spiritual paths, and they cannot all be uni-
fied and reduced to some one set of rules and regulations. But we
have already distinguished a certain form of spiritual endeavor
that emphasizes an authentically religious attitude toward man.
Here certain general presuppositions are possible. Spiritual asceticism here consists in the most open, unequivocal, and conscious
renunciation of oneself, in a readiness always to follow the will
of God, in a desire to become the fulfiller of God's design in the
world, a tool in His hands, a means and not an end. The principle
of service, of a certain spiritual mobilization, must be realized

here to the end, must embrace all of man's spiritual possibilities and forces.

In turning to the other, to the one whom he is called to serve, man cannot replace everything in the spiritual area by choosing only the highest spiritual qualities. Here begins what is most difficult and demands the maximum ascetic effort and attention. In turning his spiritual world toward the spiritual world of another, a man encounters the terrible, inspiring mystery of the authentic knowledge of God, because what he encounters is not flesh and blood, not feelings and moods, but the authentic image of God in man, the very incarnate icon of God in the world, a glimmer of the mystery of the Incarnation and Godmanhood.[11] And man must unconditionally and unreservedly accept this terrible Revelation of God, must bow down before the image of God in his brother. And only when he feels it, sees it, and understands it, will yet another mystery be revealed to him, which demands of him his most strenuous struggle, his greatest ascetic ascent. He will see how this image of God is obscured, distorted by an evil power. He will see the human heart, where the devil wages a ceaseless struggle with God. And in the name of the image of God, darkened by the devil, in the name of the love for this image of God that pierces his heart, he will want to begin a struggle with the devil, to become an instrument of God in this terrible and scorching work. He will be able to do it if all his hope is in God and not in himself; he will be able to do it if he has not a single subtle or mercenary desire; if he lays down his armor like David and with nothing but the name of God rushes to do battle with Goliath.

These briefly are the landmarks that the human soul wants to go by if it longs for ascetic endeavor in the area of its relation to people. It can all be expressed in one eternal image of the crucified Christ: He gave His flesh to be crucified, He suffered in His human soul, He gave His spirit into the hands of the Father — and He calls us to do the same. And He offered His sacrifice for the whole man, in his whole spiritual-inner-bodily composition.

There is another image that is particularly close to Orthodox consciousness — the image of the Mother who stood by the Cross of her crucified Son, the image of her to whom it was said: "Yea, a sword shall pierce thy own soul also" (Lk 2:35). This image is the great symbol of any genuine relation to man: in the Crucified she saw both God and her son, and by that she teaches us to see God — that is, the image of God — in every brother in the flesh of the Son of Man, who is also a son we adopt through our love, our compassion, our participation in his suffering, our bearing of his sins and lapses. To this day the Mother of God is pierced by the Cross of her Son, which becomes for her a two-edged sword, and by the swords of our crosses, the crosses of all Godmanhood. And, contemplating her super-worldly intercession for all human sins and weaknesses, we find in her a sure and true path that tells us to receive in our hearts the crosses of our brothers, to be pierced by them as by a weapon that pierces the soul.

Thus, the covenant of the Son of God, given to mankind, repeated many times in the Gospel, sealed by the whole endeavor of His earthly life, coincides with the covenant of the Mother of God, revealed to us since the day of the Annunciation, since the time of her terrible standing by the Cross, and through all the centuries of the Church's existence. Here there is no doubt; here the path is clear and open.

If Orthodoxy, owing to historical circumstances, occasionally adopted certain tendencies that are foreign to it, a somewhat excessive emphasis on the path of self-salvation more characteristic of the religions of the East, even through them we always see that the fundamental covenant of Christ was never forgotten or set aside. The commandment of love for one's neighbor, the second and equal in value to the first, calls mankind in the same way today as when it was first given.

For us Russian Orthodox people it may be easier to understand than for anyone else, because it was precisely this commandment that captivated and interested Russian religious thought. Without it, Khomiakov would have been unable to speak of the *sobornost'* of the Orthodox Church, which rests entirely on love, on lofty human communion. His theology shows clearly that the universal Church itself is, first of all, the incarnation not only of the commandment of the love of God, but also of love for one's neighbor, and is as unthinkable without the second as without the first.

Without the second commandment there would be no sense in Soloviev's teaching about Godmanhood, because it becomes one and organic, the genuine Body of Christ, only when united and brought to life by the flow of fraternal love that unites everyone at one Cup and brings everyone to partake of one Divine Love.

Only this commandment makes clear Dostoevsky's words about each of us being guilty for all, and each of us being answerable for each other's sins.

It can be said that for more than a century now Russian thought has been repeating with all its voices and in all possible ways that it has understood what it means to give one's soul for one's neighbors, that it wants to follow the path of love, the path of authentic mystical human communion, which is thereby also true communion with God. It has often happened in the history of thought that theoretical, philosophical, and theological presuppositions emerge first, but after that a certain idea strives to embody itself in life. All Russian spiritual works of the nineteenth century were filled with theoretical suppositions, the whole world heard them, they proved to be humanly brilliant, they determined the highest point of tension of the Russian spirit, its main characteristic. No wars or revolutions can destroy what has been done by Russian religious and philosophical genius over the course of the previous period in the history of Russian thought. Dostoevsky remains forever, and not only he. We can draw from these works, we can get from them an inestimable amount of data, answers to the most terrible questions, the posing of the most insoluble problems. One may boldly say that the main theme of nineteenth-century Russian thought had to do with the second commandment, with its dogmatic, moral, philosophical, social, and other aspects.

For us, for Orthodox people who are in the Church, and who were brought up on this Orthodox philosophy of the Russian people, our duty reveals itself with the utmost clarity: we must turn these theoretical presuppositions, these philosophical systems, these theological theories, these words *sobornost'* and

Godmanhood, which have recently become sacred, into so many practical landmarks both for our personal spiritual paths, the most cherished, most inward ones, and for any of our external endeavors.

We are called to embody in life the principles of *sobornost'* and Godmanhood, which are at the foundation of our Orthodox Church; we are called to oppose the mystery of authentic human communion to all false relations among people. This is the only path on which Christ's love can live; moreover, this is the only path of life — outside it is death. Death in the fire and ashes of various hatreds that corrode modern mankind, class, national, and race hatreds, the godless and giftless death of cool, uncreative, imitative, essentially secular democracy. To all forms of mystical totalitarianism we oppose only one thing: the person, the image of God in man. And to all forms of passively collectivist mentality in democracy we oppose *sobornost'.*

But we do not even oppose. We simply want to live as we are taught by the second commandment of Christ, which determines everything in man's relation to this earthly life, and we want to live this life in such a way that all those who are outside it can see and feel the unique, saving, unsurpassable beauty, the indisputable truth of precisely this Christian path.

We do not know whether we will be able to realize our hopes. It is basically a matter of God's will. But apart from God's will, God's help and grace, each of us is faced with the demand to strain all our forces, not fearing the most difficult endeavor, in ascetic self-restraint, giving our souls for others sacrificially and lovingly, to follow in Christ's footsteps to our appointed Golgotha.

2

On the Imitation
of the Mother of God

No gentle reflection on Mary, instead this essay is a radical state-ment about the Christian calling to imitate the Mother of God in the sharing of her Son's passion. We accomplish this by our own suffering, by carrying the cross of the neighbor's pain, and being pierced by it as a sword. Nature and common sense bid us to feel sorry about the sufferings of others, but to leave it there. A certain kind of individualistic religiosity — concerned only with "God and my soul" — makes us detached from others' pain. Mother Maria calls these tendencies "sins against the cross of God and against human crosses, sins of not admitting them into our hearts as two-edged swords." The examples of Christ and His Mother lead us beyond what is reasonable, safe, and comfortable, into the way of perfect love and perfect freedom.

We must seek authentic and profound religious bases in order to understand and justify our yearning for man, our love of man, our path among our brothers, among people.

And warnings sound from two different sides. On one side, the humanistic world, even as it accepts the foundations of Christian morality in inter-human relations, simply does not need any fur-ther deepening, any justification that does not come from itself. This world keeps within three dimensions, and with those three dimensions it exhausts the whole of existence. On the other side, the world connected with the Church also warns us: often the very theme of man seems something secondary to it, something that removes us from the one primary thing, from an authentic communion with God. For this world, Christianity is this relation to God. The rest is christianizing or christianification.

We must be deaf to these two warnings. We must not only suppose, we must know that the first of them, coming from a world deprived of God, destroys the very idea of man, who is nothing if he is not the image of God, while the second destroys the idea of the Church, which is nothing if it does not imply the individual human being within it, as well as the whole of mankind.

We must not only be deaf to these warnings, we must be convinced that the question of an authentic and profound religious attitude toward man is precisely the meeting point of all questions of the Christian and the godless world, and that even this godless world is waiting for a word from Christianity, the only word capable of healing and restoring all, and perhaps sometimes even of raising what is dead.

But at the same time, perhaps for centuries now, the Christian soul has been suffering from a sort of mystical Protestantism. Only the combination of two words carries full weight for it: God and I, God and my soul, and my path, and my salvation. For the modern Christian soul it is easier and more natural to say "My Father" than "Our Father," "deliver me from the evil one," "give me this day my daily bread," and so on.

And on these paths of the solitary soul striving toward God, it seems that everything has been gone through, all roads have been measured, all possible dangers have been accounted for, the depths of all abysses are known. It is easy to find a guide here, be it the ancient authors of ascetic books, or the modern followers of ancient ascetic traditions, who are imbued with their teachings.

But there is also a path that seeks a genuinely religious relation to people, that does not want either a humanistic simplification of human relations or an ascetic disdain of them.

Before speaking of this path, we must understand what that part of man's religious life which is exhausted by the words "God and my soul" is based on in its mystical depths.

If we decide responsibly and seriously to make the Gospel truth the standard for our human souls, we will have no doubts about how to act in any particular case of our lives: we should renounce everything we have, take up our cross, and follow Him. The only thing Christ leaves us is the path that follows after Him, and the cross which we bear on our shoulders, imitating His bearing of the cross to Golgotha.

It can be generally affirmed that Christ calls us to imitate Him. That is the exhaustive meaning of all Christian morality. And however differently various peoples in various ages understand the meaning of this imitation, all ascetic teachings in Christianity finally boil down to it. Desert dwellers imitate Christ's forty-day sojourn in the desert. Fasters fast because He fasted. The prayerful pray, following His example; virgins observe purity, and so on. It is not by chance that Thomas à Kempis entitled his book *The Imitation of Christ;* it is a universal precept of Christian morality, the common title, as it were, of all Christian asceticism.

I will not try to characterize here the different directions this imitation has taken, and its occasional deviations, perhaps, from what determines the path of the Son of Man in the Gospel. There are as many different interpretations as there are people, and deviations are inevitable, because the human soul is sick with sin and deathly weakness.

What matters is something else. What matters is that in all these various paths Christ Himself made legitimate this solitary standing of the human soul before God, this rejection of all the rest — that is, of the whole world: father and mother, as the Gospel precisely puts it, and not only the living who are close to us, but also the recently dead — everything, in short. Naked, solitary, freed of everything, the soul sees only His image before it, takes the cross on its shoulders, following His example, and goes after him to accept its own dawnless night of Gethsemane, its own terrible Golgotha, and through it to bear its faith in the Resurrection into the undeclining joy of Easter. Here it indeed seems that everything is exhausted by the words "God and my soul." All the rest is what He called me to renounce, and so there is nothing else: God — and my soul — and nothing.

No, not quite nothing. The human soul does not stand empty-handed before God. The fullness is this: God — and my soul — and the cross that it takes up. There is also the cross.

The meaning and significance of the cross are inexhaustible. The cross of Christ is the eternal tree of life, the invincible force, the union of heaven and earth, the instrument of a shameful death. But what is the cross in our path of the imitation of Christ; how should our crosses resemble the one cross of the Son of Man? For even on Golgotha there stood not one but three crosses: the cross of the God-man and the crosses of the two thieves. Are these two crosses not symbols, as it were, of all human crosses, and does it not depend on us which one we choose? For us the way of the cross is unavoidable in any case, we can only choose to freely follow either the way of the blaspheming thief and perish, or the way of the one who called upon Christ and be with Him today in paradise. For a certain length of time, the thief who chose perdition shared the destiny of the Son of Man. He was condemned and nailed to a cross in the same way; he suffered torment in the same way. But that does not mean that his cross was the imitation of Christ's cross, that his path led him in the footsteps of Christ.

What is most essential, most determining in the image of the cross is the necessity of freely and voluntarily accepting it and taking it up. Christ freely, voluntarily took upon Himself the sins of the world, and raised them up on the cross, and thereby redeemed them and defeated hell and death. To accept the endeavor and the responsibility voluntarily, to freely crucify your sins — that is the meaning of the cross, when we speak of bearing it on our human paths. Freedom is the inseparable sister of responsibility. The cross is this freely accepted responsibility, clear-sighted and sober.

In taking the cross on his shoulders, man renounces everything — and that means that he ceases to be part of this whole natural world. He ceases to submit to its natural laws, which free the human soul from responsibility. Natural laws not only free one from responsibility, they also deprive one of freedom.

Indeed, what sort of responsibility is it, if I act as the invincible laws of my nature dictate, and where is the freedom, if I am entirely under the law?

And so the Son of Man showed his brothers in the flesh a supra-natural — and in this sense not a human but a Godmanly — path of freedom and responsibility. He told them that the image of God in them also makes them into God-men and calls them to be deified, to indeed become Sons of God, freely and responsibly taking their crosses on their shoulders.

The free path to Golgotha — that is the true imitation of Christ.

This would seem to exhaust all the possibilities of the Christian soul, and thus the formula "God and my soul" indeed embraces the whole world. All the rest that was renounced on the way appears only as a sort of obstacle adding weight to my cross. And heavy as it may be, whatever human sufferings it may place on my shoulders, it is all the same *my* cross, which determines *my* personal way to God, *my* personal following in the footsteps of Christ. My illness, my grief, my loss of dear ones, my relations to people, to my vocation, to my work — these are details of *my* path, not ends in themselves, but a sort of grindstone on which my soul is sharpened, certain — perhaps sometimes burdensome — exercises for my soul, the particularities of my personal path.

If that is so, it certainly settles the question. It can only be endlessly varied, depending on the individual particularities of epochs, cultures, and separate persons. But essentially everything is clear. God and my soul, bearing its cross. In this an enormous spiritual freedom, activity, and responsibility are confirmed. And that is all.

I think it is Protestant mysticism that should follow such a path most consistently. Moreover, in so far as the world now lives the mystical life, it is for the most part infected by this isolating and individualistic Protestant mysticism. In it there is, of course, no place for the Church, for the principle of *sobornost'*, for the God-manly perception of the whole Christian process. There are simply millions of people born into the world, some of whom hear Christ's call to renounce everything, take up their cross, and follow Him, and, as far as their strength, their faith, their personal endeavor allow, they answer that call. They are saved by it, they meet Christ, as if merging their life with His. All the rest is a sort of humanistic afterthought, a sort of adjusting of these basic Christian principles to those areas of life that lie outside them. In short, some sort of christianification, not bad in essence, but deprived of all true mystical roots, and therefore not inevitably necessary.

The cross of Golgotha is the cross of the Son of Man, the crosses of the thieves and our personal crosses are precisely personal, and as an immense forest of these personal crosses we are moving along the paths to the Kingdom of Heaven. And that is all.

•

Not so long ago I happened to visit a military cemetery. An enormous space was filled with hundreds of neat graves, tightly packed together, row after row. Over each grave was a cross — no, not a cross but a cross-like sword, the blade stuck in the ground, the hilt as if forming the crossbar. The cross had become a sword, or the sword a cross. This merging of the cross and the sword is known from the Middle Ages. They deliberately made the crossbar thick to resemble a cross, and relics were enshrined in the hilt. Besides that, I also remembered the journalistic combining of these two short, enormous words. Many people have played on this combination, covering over the pathos of war, justifying its violence. Be that as it may, the combination, the tendency to merge the sword and the cross, is not a rare thing.

And in a unique and quite different sense, we also find this combination in the Gospel. "Yea, a sword shall pierce thy own soul also" (Lk 2:35). The two-edged sword of the Mother of God. This is a first distinction from the usual combination, and the most essential one. When our journalists say "the cross and the sword," they imply that the cross is passive suffering, while the sword for them is a symbol of activity. Not so in the Gospel. The cross is taken up voluntarily, and therefore actively, by the Son of Man. The sword deals a blow, it pierces the soul, which passively receives it. According to the Gospel, the sword is a symbol of suffering endured passively, not voluntarily chosen but inevitable — a weapon that pierces the soul. The cross of the Son of Man, accepted voluntarily, becomes a two-edged sword that pierces the soul of the Mother, not because she voluntarily chooses it, but because she cannot help suffering the sufferings of her Son.

And this two-edged sword is not uniquely and unrepeatably bound up with the destiny of the Mother of God alone — it teaches all of us something and obliges us to something. To understand that, we need to feel the Mother of God's earthly path, to see all that is both exceptional and universal in it.

Orthodox consciousness always bears in its depths the mystery of the Mother of God. For it, she is not only the suffering Mother at the cross of her crucified Son, she is also the Queen of Heaven, "more honorable than the cherubim and more glorious beyond compare than the seraphim." Orthodox consciousness understands her, the Virgin of the tribe of Judah, the daughter of David, as the Mother of all that lives, as the living and personal incarnation of the Church, as the human Body of Christ. The veil of the Mother of God protects the world, and she is also the "moist mother earth."[12] This last image acquires new strength in connection with thoughts of the cross that becomes a two-edged sword. The earth of Golgotha with the cross set up on it, piercing it, the earth of Golgotha red with blood — is it not a mother's heart pierced by a sword? The cross of Golgotha, like a sword, pierces the soul of Mother-earth.

And if we turn away from what is revealed to us in the glorified image of the Mother of God, if we take her only in her earthly path, that is, where it is possible to speak of "imitating" her, that is quite enough to enable a Christian soul to understand some of the special possibilities opened up to it. It is precisely on this path of God-motherhood that we must seek the justification and substantiation of our hopes, and find the religious and mystical meaning of true human communion, which otherwise somehow escapes us.

We may affirm directly that the authentic religious attitude toward man, in all its scope, with all its particular and personal details, only reveals itself fully when it is sanctified by the path of the Mother of God, is guided in her footsteps. Is illumined by her.

And here the most important thing is to feel what the Son's Golgotha is for the Mother.

He endures His voluntary suffering on the cross — she involuntarily co-suffers with Him. He bears the sins of the world — she collaborates with him, she co-participates, she co-feels, co-experiences. His flesh is crucified — she is co-crucified.

Let us not measure the degree of suffering on Golgotha. Its measure is given to us: the cross of the Son, in all its scope, in all its pain, becomes a two-edged sword that pierces the maternal heart. These two torments are equally measureless. The only difference is that the Son's active, voluntary, and willing acceptance becomes the Mother's passive, unavoidable co-acceptance.

On Golgotha, the words of the Annunciation — "Behold the handmaid of the Lord" (Lk 1:38) — do not sound triumphant; the thought that "all generations shall call me blessed" (Lk 1:48) is muted in them. On Golgotha she is the handmaid of her suffering God-Son, the handmaid of His sufferings. It is the same obedience as on the day of the Good News, the same co-participation in the Divine economy, but then it was the path toward the Nativity, toward co-participation in the angelic song: "Glory to God in the highest, and on earth peace, good will toward men" (Lk 2:14), while now it is participation in the suffering of Golgotha, the kenosis of God, inevitable from all eternity. The rocks split, the earth cracked open, the curtain of the temple was torn in two, the Mother's soul was pierced by the sword of the cross, the Son gave up His spirit into the hands of the Father.

Of course, the Mother of God had her own destiny, her own cross. But can her destiny be called a cross that was voluntarily chosen and taken up? It seems to me that her destiny was the cross of her Son become a sword that pierced her soul.

Her whole mystery lies in this co-uniting with the destiny of her Son, from the Annunciation and the Nativity, through

Golgotha, to the Resurrection, to Pentecost, to the eternal heavenly glorification of the Dormition.

Always — His will be done — the handmaid of God is open to His fate, to His piercing cross.

So it was in the hour of Golgotha, in the thirty-third year of our era — and so it will be eternally. Eternal is the Golgotha of the Son of Man, eternal are His sufferings on the cross, and eternal are the sufferings from the sword that pierces the Mother's heart.

There is much in this maternal suffering that we can perceive and learn today, drawing conclusions with regard to our own human suffering.

First and foremost, we see Christ's humanity, the Church of Christ, the Body of Christ, of which the Mother of God is also the Mother. And this expression is not merely a sort of pious lyricism; it corresponds precisely to the understanding of the Church as the Body of Christ. And if so, then what she felt in relation to her Son is as eternally alive in relation to the Church. As the Mother of Godmanhood — the Church — she is pierced even now by the suffering of this Body of Christ, the suffering of each member of this Body. In other words, all the countless crosses that mankind takes on its shoulders to follow Christ also become countless swords eternally piercing her maternal heart. She continues to *co*-participate, *co*-feel, *co*-suffer with each human soul, as then on Golgotha.

That is foremost. And in this sense she always walks with us on our own way of the cross, she is always there beside us, each of our crosses is a sword for her.

But there is another thing, no less essential. Every man is not only the image of God, the icon of the Divinity, not only a brother in the flesh of the God-man, deified by Him, and honored by His cross, and in this sense a son of the Mother of God. Every man is also the image of the Mother of God, who bears Christ in herself through the Holy Spirit. In this sense, every man deep inside is this bi-une icon of the Mother of God with the Child, the revelation of this bi-une mystery of Godmanhood. This can easily be seen simply by following how Old Testament mankind

was preparing itself for the divine birth, how all of God's promises come down precisely to this promise of the divine birth. And
the Virgin Mary was in full measure bound up with this hoped-
for divine birth from the house of David, the tribe of Judah, the
seed of Abraham. And we, the Church of the New Testament,
which grew out of the Old, have lost nothing in this area. In this
sense we can speak of the physical participation of mankind —
and therefore of every separate man — in the birth of the Son
of God. But of this we can and must speak at the deepest, most
mystical level of human souls. And, finally, an analysis of the verbal equation "Son of God — Son of Man" gives proof of the
God-bearing of man.

Thus the human soul unites in itself two images — the image
of the Son of God and the image of the Mother of God — and
thereby should participate not only in the destiny of the Son, but
also in her destiny. Both the Son of God and His Mother are
age-old archetypes, symbols by which the soul orients itself on its
religious paths. In this sense it should imitate not only Christ but
also the Mother of God. This means it should accept and take up
not only its freely chosen cross; it should also know the mystery
of the cross that becomes a sword. First of all, the cross of the
Son of Man on Golgotha should pierce every Christian soul like
a sword, should be experienced by it as a co-participation, a co-
suffering with Him. Besides that, it should also accept the swords
of its brothers' crosses.

Indeed, let us try to examine more subtly and distinctly the
covenant of the path of the divine motherhood of the human
soul, in which every man participates to some degree.

If a man is not only the image of God but also the image of the
Mother of God, then he should also be able to see the image of
God and the image of the Mother of God in every other man. In
man's God-motherly soul not only is the birth of the Son of God
announced and Christ born, but there also develops the keen perception of Christ's image in other souls. And in this sense, the
God-motherly part of the human soul begins to see other people
as its children; it adopts them for itself. The limit of the God-
motherly relation is the perceiving of God and Son in the other,

a limit which, of course, could have been reached only by the Virgin Mary. But insofar as we must strive to follow her path, and as her image is the image of our human soul, so we must also perceive God and Son in every man. God, because he is the image and likeness of God; the Son, because as it gives birth to Christ within itself, the human soul thereby adopts the whole Body of Christ for itself, the whole of Godmanhood, and every man individually.

Let the cross lie on human shoulders, along the path of human God-likeness. The human heart should also be pierced by the two-edged swords, the soul-cutting weapons, of other people's crosses. Our neighbor's cross should be a sword that pierces our soul. Our soul should co-participate in its neighbor's destiny, co-feel, co-suffer. And it is not the soul that chooses these swords; they are chosen by those who took them up like a cross on their shoulders. After the likeness of its archetype, the Mother of God, the human soul is drawn to Golgotha in the footsteps of her son, and cannot help being drawn there, cannot help bleeding.

To my mind, it is here that the authentic mystical bases of human communion lie.

And we should not be disturbed by the ostensibly proud and arrogant assertion that our souls are related in a motherly way to other people's souls. A mother is not greater than her children, and often is even lesser. And maternity does not mean either spiritual age or the measure of an endeavor — it expresses only a humble and obedient striving to participate in another's Golgotha, to open one's heart to the stroke of the two-edged sword. It can all be said more simply and in a single word. Maternity means love.

Our relation to man should not be like a sort of extra burden that increases the burden of our own crosses, not like a pious exercise, a duty, the development of a virtue.

Only one single law exists here. Our relation is determined only by seeing the image of God in him, and, on the other hand, in adopting him as a son. Here duty, virtue, pious exercise — it all fades away.

The first founder of the deed of love teaches us the humble acceptance of these other crosses. She calls every Christian soul to repeat tirelessly after her: "Behold the handmaid of the Lord," even to shedding one's blood, even to feeling as if a sword has pierced one's heart.

This is the measure of love; this is the limit to which the human soul should aspire. We can even say that this is the only proper relation of one person to another. Only when one's soul takes up another person's cross, his doubts, his grief, his temptations, falls, sins — only then is it possible to speak of a proper relation to another.

And just as the only proper bearing of the cross in the world was Christ's bearing of the cross, so the only proper acceptance of the piercing sword was the acceptance of the Mother who stood by the cross on Golgotha. In this lies the uniqueness of His holiness. In this also lies her eternal, unattainable holiness. And if so, then any other relation to the cross and the sword is a sin, in various degrees, from the rare falling away and weakening of the Christian path in the consciousness of ascetics to a complete and wholesale rejection of it.

And so here, on this path of God-motherhood, we must sort out our sins. Naturally, they will all be sins against man — as God-like and as adopted son; they will be sins against the cross of God and against human crosses, sins of not admitting them into our hearts as two-edged swords.

It goes without saying that it seems to every man as if nothing will be left of his heart, that it will bleed itself dry, if he opens it, not for the countless swords of all Godmanhood, but even for the one sword of the nearest and dearest of his brothers. It is hard to object to that. It is hard to deny the legitimacy and naturalness of a certain inner self-defense of the human soul against all sorts of unnecessary burdens that beset it. It is hard on the level of natural law. And natural law, which in some false way has penetrated into the supernatural law of spiritual life, will say definitively: bear your cross responsibly, freely, and honestly, opening your heart now and then to the cross-swords of your neighbors — and that is all.

But if the cross of Christ is a scandal or a folly for natural law, then the two-edged weapon that pierces the soul should be as much of a folly and as much of a scandal for it. Yet for Christians not only the cross but the cross that becomes a sword must, without any reservations, without any attempt at a reasonable assessment of one's own powers, be God's power and God's Wisdom. What's more, all that is not the fullness of cross-bearing, and all that is not the fullness of swords received in one's heart, is sin.

And if, with this measure of sin, we begin to test our attitudes toward people, we will see that each of them is sinful. Our attitude toward those who are far from us, whom we cannot perceive as the image of God and make no attempt to adopt, is thoroughly sinful. Sinful, too, is our attitude toward those whom we seem to serve and help, but without being wounded by them, without feeling the whole force of their cross as a weapon that pierces our soul. Sinful, finally, is our attitude toward those who are closest to us, whom we do sometimes perceive in the full measure of the proper attitude — that is, we are pierced by their crosses, we see the image of God in them and adopt them, but we do it in some special moments of their life and our own, and afterwards lapse again into a natural, that is, a sinful, indifference to them. Sinful, finally, is our attitude toward the Man of men, toward the Son of Man, because we rarely perceive His cross, too, as a weapon that pierces our soul.

And what hinders us? What makes all our human communion inwardly sinful and depraved? That we are guided on our spiritual paths by the measure of natural law, and calculate our natural forces, forgetting that on the Christian path our forces are supernatural — and therefore inexhaustible. We may say exactly that we are hindered by poverty of faith.

In the Christian life there should be not only the holy folly[13] of the cross, but also the holy folly of the sword, not only the crucifixion of the self, but also the co-crucifixion of oneself, the standing on Golgotha, at the foot of every human cross. The Christian soul should be filial, that is, cross-bearing, but also maternal, that is, receptive of the sword in the heart.

It is frightening to look at one's life, testing it by faithfulness to the cross-sword. All we see is falling away, betrayal, coldness, and indifference. Each relation with a person is only sin, always sin. Always according to the laws of this world, never according to the image of God. And cunning reason confirms the inevitability of natural law, the excessiveness, the unbearableness of the cross, the excessiveness of the sword. How can we make it so that the word of the cross is neither folly nor scandal?

The Son of God, the eternal archetype of every human soul, prayed to His Father: "Thy will be done." And the words of the Mother spoke of the same thing: "Behold the handmaid of the Lord." And we also find that in the innermost depths of our human hearts, God-like and maternal in their spiritual essence.

That gives us some strength, not that it delivers us from sin with regard to God and people, but in that we at least feel this sin as sin, and not as a legitimate and natural state justified by reason and nature.

3

The Mysticism
of Human Communion

*As crucial as it is for Christians to face the world, its needs,
and sufferings, it is even more necessary that social action —
the service of the neighbor — be properly grounded. The proper
foundation will be the love of God, for then each suffering
brother and sister will be recognized as made in God's image
and likeness; truly in each neighbor will be visible the face of
Christ. This is Mother Maria's essential view of her work of
"loving kindness."*

The most doubtful, disputable, and unsatisfying thing about all
the concepts of "Christianity turned toward the world," "social
Christianity," and similar trends that have been put forward in
modern times, is their secondary character, their incommensura-
bility with the idea of Christian life understood as communion
with God. Something of the "second sort," applied, appended, is
not bad in itself, but is also not necessary — and in any case cannot exhaust the fullness of Christian life. Primary Christianity, on
the other hand, exhausts everything, because it is oriented toward
authentic spiritual life, that is, toward communion with God. In
this characterization there is undoubtedly a portion of truth, because all the trends of social Christianity known to us are based
on a certain rationalistic humanism, apply only the principle of

Christian morality to "this world," and do not seek a spiritual and mystical basis for their constructions.

To make social Christianity not only Christian-like but truly Christian, it is necessary to find one more dimension for it, to bring it out of flat soulfulness and two-dimensional moralism into the depths of multi-dimensional spirituality. To substantiate it mystically and spiritually. It seems to me that this coincides precisely with what Orthodoxy — which has not yet spoken in this area — can and must say; it will give greater depth to Catholic and Protestant attempts to turn a Christian face to the world.

•

An extraordinary similarity of extremes can be observed in regard to the question of the world. On the one hand, worldly people are essentially separated from the world by an impenetrable wall. However much they give themselves to the joys of the world, whatever bustle they live in, there is always an impassable abyss in their consciousness: "I" and the world, which serves me, amuses me, grieves me, wearies me, and so on. The more egoistic a man is, that is, the more he belongs to the world, the more alienated he is from the authentic life of the world, the more the world is some sort of inanimate comfort for him, or some sort of inanimate torture, to which his uniquely animate "I" is opposed. If he loves the world, science, art, nature, family, friends, politics, it is with what may be called lustful love — "my family," "my art," "my nature," "my politics." All this reveals, embodies, reflects, realizes a single excessive "I." In this relation to the world there exist insuperable, high walls that separate man from man, nature, and God.

We may boldly say that the most worldly man is the most separated and disconnected from the life of the world. But in Christianity, where two God-given commandments — about the love of God and the love of man — should resound, we often run into the same separation from man and from the world. It would seem that a Christian cannot say: "I love God, and therefore man is indifferent for me." The apostle John answers him severely: "Hypocrite, how can you love God whom you have not seen, if you scorn your brother who is near to you?" (cf. 1 Jn 4:20). But even if the Christian does not put it so crudely, still there is a certain possibility of harming one's love of man because of one's love of God. Love of God — that is the chief and only thing. All the rest is just obedience, just a "job," which in any case should not diminish the chief thing. As a result, man has his own monastery — in his spirit, behind high white walls. There he abides in the fullness and purity of his communion with God, and from there, by way of some sort of condescension, some sort of patronizing, he descends into the sinful and suffering world. He fulfills his duty of obedience before it, a duty that has a very strict and precise boundary. It must not disturb the inner rhythm of his life in God, a certain sacred comfort; it must not captivate him in the depths of his spirit, because in those depths abides the divine Holy of Holies. Pity, love, work, responsibility for the human soul, willingness to sacrifice — these are all necessary elements of obedience, but one must know moderation in them. They should not be allowed to overwhelm and disperse the spirit. Compared to the chief thing, it is all not a deed but a job. Otherwise one might lose one's "I," scatter it through the world. This "I" is, in a certain sense, opposed to the world. And the world either simply lies in evil, or is the field where we exercise our virtues — in any case, it is outside the "I." Separation from the world occurs on different principles here than with worldly people, but it is no less complete for all that. In this isolation of the "I" from the world, opposites meet.

Here we must add the reservation that there is, of course, work that can essentially be called a "job." When hermits wove mats and fashioned clay pots, it was a job. When we peel potatoes, mend underwear, do the accounts, ride the subway, that is also a job. But when the monks of old, by way of obedience, buried the dead, looked after lepers, preached to fallen women, denounced the unrighteous life, gave alms — that was not a job. And when we act in our modern life, visiting the sick, feeding the unemployed, teaching children, keeping company with all kinds of human grief and failure, dealing with drunkards, criminals, madmen, the dejected, the gone-to-seed, with all the spiritual leprosy of our life, it is not a job and not only a tribute to obedience that has its limits within our chief endeavor — it is that very inner endeavor itself, an inseparable part of our main task. The more we go out into the world, the more we give ourselves to the world, the less we are of the world, because what is of the world does not give itself to the world.

•

Let us try to substantiate this theologically, spiritually, and mystically. The great and only first founder of worldly endeavor was Christ, the Son of God, who descended into the world, became incarnate in the world, totally, entirely, without holding any reserve, as it were, for His Divinity. Did He hold back His Divinity and Himself? Was He in the world merely as the obedient Son of the Father?

In His worldly obedience He emptied Himself, and His emptying is the only example for our path. God who became a child, God who fled into Egypt to escape Herod, God who sought friends and disciples in this world, God who wept from the depths of His Spirit over Lazarus, who denounced the pharisees, who spoke of the fate of Jerusalem, who drove out demons, healed the sick, raised the dead, who finally, and most importantly, gave His Flesh and Blood as food for the world, lifted up His Body on the cross between the two thieves — when and at what moment did His example teach us about inner walls that separate us from the world? He was in the world with all His Godmanhood, not with some secondary properties. He did not keep Himself, He gave Himself without stint. "This is my Body, which is broken for you" — that is, given without stint. "This is my Blood, which is shed for you" — shed to the end. In the sacrament of the eucharist, Christ gave Himself, His God-man's Body, to the world, or rather, He united the world with Himself in the communion with his God-man's Body. He made it into Godmanhood. And it would sound almost blasphemous if He had wanted to isolate some inner, deep Christ who remained alien to this God-man's sacrifice. Christ's love does not know how to measure and divide, does not know how to spare itself. Neither did Christ teach the apostles to be sparing and cautious in love — and He could not have taught them that, because He included them in the communion of the eucharistic sacrifice, made them into the Body of Christ — and thereby gave them up to be immolated for the world. Here we need only learn and draw conclusions. It might be said paradoxically that in the sense of giving Himself to the world, Christ was the most worldly of all the sons of Adam. But we already know that what is of the world does not give itself to the world.

•

I think that the fullest understanding of Christ's giving Himself to the world, creating the one Body of Christ, Godmanhood, is contained in the Orthodox idea of *sobornost'*.[14] And *sobornost'* is not only some abstraction, on the one hand, nor is it, on the other hand, a higher reality having no inner connection with the individual human persons who constitute it: it is a higher reality because each of its members is a member of the Body of Christ, full-grown and full-fledged, because he is that "soul" which is worth the whole world. Each man, manifested to us from the moment of the first Old Testament revelations as the image of God, in Christ discloses still more strongly and concretely his connection with God. He is indeed the image of God, the image of Christ, the icon of Christ. Who, after that, can differentiate the worldly from the heavenly in the human soul, who can tell where the image of God ends and the heaviness of human flesh begins! In communing with the world in the person of each individual human being, we know that we are communing with the image of God, and, contemplating that image, we touch the Archetype — we commune with God.

There is an authentic, and truly Orthodox, mysticism not only of communion with God, but also of communion with man. And communion with man in this sense is simply another form of communion with God. In communing with people we commune not only with like-minded people, friends, co-religionists, subordinates, superiors — not only, finally, with material for our exercises in obedience and love; we commune with Christ Him-self, and only a peculiar materialism with regard to Christ's appearing and abiding in the world can explain our inability to meet Him within the bustle, in the very depth of the human fall. Here indeed the point of the matter is not only the symbol of meeting with Christ — an act limited in time — but the reality of feeling our connection with the Body of Christ, of being in Christ all the time, of associating ourselves indissolubly with Him in His God-manly abiding in the world. He foresaw our ration-alistic and proud lack of faith when He prophesied that, to his accusation, people would ask in perplexity: "Lord, when did we not visit you in the hospital or in prison, when did we refuse you a cup of water?" If they could believe that in every beggar and in every criminal Christ Himself addresses us, they would treat people differently. But the point is precisely that our communion with people passes mostly on the level of earthly encounters and is deprived of the authentic mysticism that turns it into commu-nion with God. And we are given a perfectly real possibility in our communing in love with mankind, with the world, to feel ourselves in authentic communion with Christ.

•

And this makes perfectly clear what our relations to people, to their souls, to their deeds, to human destiny, to human history as a whole should be. During a service, the priest does not only cense the icons of the Savior, the Mother of God, and the saints. He also censes the icon-people, the image of God in the people who are present. And as they leave the church precincts, these people remain as much the images of God, worthy of being censed and venerated. Our relations with people should be an authentic and profound veneration.

There are notions in Orthodoxy that attract our hearts but are not always clear to us, are not revealed to the end. We like it when the "churching" of life is discussed, but few people understand what it means. Indeed, must we attend all the church services in order to "church" our life? Or hang an icon in every room and burn an icon-lamp in front of it? No, the churching of life is the sense of the whole world as one church, adorned with icons that should be venerated, that should be honored and loved, because these icons are true images of God that have the holiness of the Living God upon them.

Just as fascinating, though enigmatic, for us is the expression "liturgy outside the church." The church liturgy and the words spoken in it give us the key for understanding this notion. We hear: "Let us love one another, that with one mind we may confess...." And further on: "Thine own of Thine own we offer unto Thee, on behalf of all and for all." These "others" whom we love with one mind in the church also work with us outside the church, rejoicing, suffering, living. And those who are His and of Him, offering unto Him on behalf of all and for all, are indeed "all," that is, all possible encounters on our way, all people sent to us by God. The wall of the church did not separate some small flock from them all. On the other hand, we believe that the eucharistic sacrament offers up the Lamb of God, the Body of Christ, as a sacrifice for the sins of the world. And, being in communion with this sacrificial Body, we ourselves become offered in sacrifice — "on behalf of all and for all." In this sense, the liturgy outside the church is our sacrificial ministry in the church of the world, adorned with living icons of God, our common ministry, an all-human sacrificial offering of love, the great act of our God-manly union, the united prayerful breath of our God-manly spirit. In this liturgical communion with people, we partake of a communion with God, we really become one flock and one Shepherd, one body, of which the inalienable head is Christ.

To clarify everything, we must make a few more reservations. Only this approach to the world and to man makes it impossible to say that the world distracts us, that man devours our concentration with his bustle. It is our own sinful distraction that distracts us and our own sinful bustle that devours our concentration. We get from the world and from man what we count on getting from them. We may get a disturbing neighbor in the same apartment, or an all-too-merry drinking companion, or a capricious and slow-witted student, or obnoxious ladies, or seedy old codgers, and so on, and relations with them will only weary us physically, annoy us inwardly, deaden us spiritually. But, through Christ's image in man, we may partake of the Body of Christ. If our approach to the world is correct and spiritual, we will not have only to give to it from our spiritual poverty, but we will receive infinitely more from the face of Christ that lives in it, from our communion with Christ, from the consciousness of being a part of Christ's body.

And it seems to me that this mysticism of human communion is the only authentic basis for any external Christian activity, for social Christianity, which in this sense has not been born yet, for a Christianity turned toward the world, and so on. Social endeavor should be just as much of a liturgy outside the church as any communion with man in the Name of Christ. Otherwise, even if it is based on Christian morals, it will merely be Christian-like, essentially secondary. Everything in the world can be Christian, but only if it is pervaded by the authentic awe of communion with God, which is also possible on the path of authentic communion with man. But outside this chief thing, there is no authentic Christianity.

Such, it seems to me, are the difficult demands Christianity must place before all attempts at building life.

•

Having begun with what is biggest and most absolute, let us throw a bridge across to our everyday destiny, to each fact of our small, concrete lives — and they are emigrant lives, which means that we cannot really talk about any great perspectives.

However, each of us is given a destiny which is no whit smaller and no less tragic because it is given us in Paris and not in Moscow. It was given each of us to be born, to love, to have friends, to thirst for creativity, to feel compassion, justice, a longing for eternity, and to each of us will be given death. We stand before the truth of the Lord and want to fulfill its commands.

And the truth of the Lord tells us that the heavens cannot contain it, but it is contained in the manger in Bethlehem; that it creates and upholds the world, and falls under the weight of the cross on the way to Golgotha; that it is more than the universe, and at the same time does not scorn a cup of water offered by a compassionate hand. The truth of the Lord abolishes the difference between the immense and the insignificant. Let us try to build our small, our insignificant life in the same way as the Great Architect builds the planetary system of the immense universe.

People make a choice between the sorrowful face of Christ and the joy of life. He who rejects the sorrowful face of Christ in the name of the joys of life believes in those joys, but tragedy is born at the moment when he discovers that those joys are not joyful. Forced, mechanized labor gives us no joy; entertainment, more or less monotonous, differing only in the degree to which it exhausts our nerves, gives us no joy; the whole of this bitter life give us no joy. Without Christ the world attains the maximum of bitterness, because it attains the maximum of meaninglessness.

Christianity is Paschal joy, Christianity is collaboration with God, Christianity is an obligation newly undertaken by mankind to cultivate the Lord's paradise, once rejected in the fall; and in the thicket of this paradise, overgrown with the weeds of many centuries of sin and the thorns of our dry and loveless life, Christianity commands us to root up, plow, sow, weed, and harvest.

Authentic, God-manly, integral, *sobornoe*[15] Christianity calls us in the Paschal song: "Let us embrace one another." In the liturgy we say, "Let us love one another, that with one mind we may confess...." Let us love — meaning not only one mind, but also one activity, meaning a common life.

It is necessary to build our relations to man and to the world not on human and worldly laws, but within the revelation of the divine commandment. To see in man the image of God and in the world God's creation. It is necessary to understand that Christianity demands of us not only the mysticism of communion with God, but also the mysticism of communion with man.

4

The Cross and
the Hammer-and-Sickle

*While the title might suggest a Christian attack on the evils
of communism, Mother Maria's response is characteristically
unusual and surprising. Having been drawn to revolutionary
politics in her youth (she was nearly executed by both the Reds
and the Whites in Russia), she knew socialism from the inside.
She was in a unique position to indicate precisely where the
revolution had gone wrong and where the Gospel could suc-
cessfully transfigure its ideals and actions, thus establishing a
civilization of freedom, justice, and love.*

The theme of this article is mainly whether it is possible, with
certain reservations, to put the conjunction "and" between the
word "cross" and the words "hammer-and-sickle," or whether
in all circumstances we must write the conjunction "or."

In our time it would seem to have become definitively clear
that there are two forces struggling in the world — the force
of Christianity and the force of godless, militant communism —
and the space between them is disappearing more and more, col-
lapsing in a total lack of will and creativity. The exclusiveness
of these two forces clearly shows their irreconcilability, their incompatibility. And thus it also seems perfectly clear that there
should be the same incompatibility between the symbols of these
forces — the cross and the hammer-and-sickle. And in fact that

is so, if we endow the hammer-and-sickle with the same conventional meaning as the communists do: the hammer-and-sickle as a symbol of the dictatorship of the proletariat, the symbol of forced happiness ushered in by iron and blood, the symbol of the absorption of the human person by an impersonal collective, the symbol of the class struggle, the symbol of leveling. To this can be added much that the communists themselves would not agree to, but that is now essentially connected with this symbol: it speaks of slavery, violence, dead bodies, the GPU, Solovki;[16] it speaks — even shouts — of the persecution of the Church, of the godless five-year plan, of everything that is directly opposed to Christian relations to life, to man, to labor, to creativity, to the historical process, to relations between classes, and so on. Thus it seems we must put the word "or" in the title of our article and consider that the theme itself, as it was originally entitled, does not exist.

And yet...and yet the world now needs, and needs urgently, an authentic idea of the hammer and the sickle purified of communist perversion. What's more, not only the world but the cross needs that this authentic idea of the hammer and the sickle be realized. In other words, it is becoming increasingly clear that the well-known words of the Internationale — "No one will grant us deliverance.... We will achieve liberation with our own hands" — are in need of essential correction. Nobody will achieve anything by his own hands.

The liberation of life from the dead end it finds itself in can proceed only from where there is a power greater than life, only from where there is the possibility of a supra-physical, supra-historical resolution of the question. Only the Church can liberate and direct our life. The Church must turn to the cry of the world, to the social hell, to injustice, crises, unemployment, and speak the words given her from all eternity: "Come unto me, all ye that labor and are heavy laden, and I will give you rest" (Mt 11:28). These are the only hands that can actually grant deliverance, that can sanctify man's path and re-fashion the hammer-and-sickle into a symbol of labor in Christ's name — labor in the fields of the Lord.

And so, a first point: only in Christ's name can we do the one thing that needs to be done to the world — lead it out of the dead end of contemporary godless fruitlessness and giftlessness. By the name of Christ, by the cross of Christ, the hammer-and-sickle can be given their authentic meaning; by the cross labor can be sanctified and blessed. "And" not only can but should stand between the words "Church" and "labor," "cross" and "hammer-and-sickle."

The difficulty here is not in the principle. Remove the violent, Bolshevik approach to the matter, and everything will be simple. In principle, the cross should be combined with labor.

The complication is that yet another very important and decisive question arises. The cross should be combined with labor, but that is possible only in the presence of one further possibility: if it is proved that the symbol of the hammer-and-sickle can be purified of violence and coercion, if labor can be free and voluntarily chosen. This condition is inevitable, because Christ, the cross, and the Church can in no circumstances go hand in hand with anything that contains an element of violence and servitude. Therefore it is quite impossible, for instance, to speak of a christianization of communism. The christianization of communism implies the destruction of its very heart: its coercion, its violence, the dictatorship of the proletariat, the party hegemony of selective communist rule.

Christ is freedom: the face of Christ is the affirmation in every person of his own free and God-like face; the Church is a free and organic union of the faithful with Christ, with Christ's freedom; and Christ calls those who labor and are heavy laden to take up His burden, which is light because it is taken up freely. Thus Christ and coercion are incompatible. If in our time the principle of labor is inevitably combined with coercion, with dictatorship, with blood and iron, then indeed it is not to be combined with the cross, and between the words "cross" and "hammer-and-sickle" we must indeed put the disjunctive little word "or."

How easy and simple it is to prove with very convincing arguments the possibility of free labor and of the free construction of society on the principle of labor! In fact, mankind has enough experience of the two opposite systems of coercion and violence. The old coercion of the capitalist regime, which destroys the right to life and leaves one only with the right to labor, has recently begun to deprive people of that right as well. Forced crisis, forced unemployment, forced labor, joyless and with no inner justification — enough of all that. But try going to the opposite system. It turns out to be the system of communist enforcement: the same joyless labor under the rod, well-organized slavery, violence, hunger — enough of that, too. It is clear to everybody that we must seek a path to free, purposeful, and expedient labor, that we must take the world as a sort of garden that it is incumbent upon us to cultivate. Who doubts that?

And it is here that the major temptation, the most tormenting doubt, arises, the more convincing as it rests not only on
principles but also on our concrete life experience.

An eternal argument begins between the free truth of Christ
and a certain other principle, so wisely and accurately shown by
Dostoevsky.

This other principle has many shapes in Dostoevsky: first, ancient Rome, the great and forcedly organized human anthill; then
the Grand Inquisitor, who by coercion implants happiness everywhere and removes responsibility, that is, freedom, from human
souls; finally, Shigalyov and Shigalyovism,[17] the demonism of
Demons, the leveling of mountains, the turning of mankind into
a well-fed and contented herd, obliged to labor, true, but to make
up for it, free of all responsibility.

So it was in Dostoevsky's day. In our time the great Shigalyov has become incarnate. In our day, he acts under pseudonyms
of world renown. First it was "Lenin," now it is "Stalin,"
"communist power," "the general party line."

On becoming incarnate, he has turned out to have a greater
number of flaws than the theoretical Shigalyov of Dostoevsky.
The latter promised the human herd food and contentment. This
one keeps people half starved. But the principle here is the same
as ever — a coercively introduced system of values.

Christ, in giving us His free path and His freely chosen burden,
thereby confirmed, as it were, the possibility of a belief in human
freedom and in the divine dignity of the human face.

And we? Do we believe in that freedom? Do we believe in
that dignity? Not only in someone else, but in ourselves, each in
himself? It is very hard to answer this question positively, much
though we want this positive answer. On the contrary, there is a
great deal of evidence for a negative answer.

In each of us sits a small inquisitor, a small Shigalyov, and
a small general party line, because we ourselves wait to be co-
erced and willingly apply this coercion in setting up our system
of life among others. And that is not even our main trouble, but
that these others in their attitude toward freedom and coercion
nourish our inner Shigalyovism.

What am I talking about? About the most terrible thing that exists in earthly life, in the historical process, in the throbbing of modernity: that no one, no one wants in a voluntary and friendly, free and brotherly fashion to build an authentic, laboring, free, and loving Christian life. If they do build, they build something different, and if there is something that is not different, it is not in the building of life, but always in words and theories, sometimes quite remarkable, but only words and theories.

As a pianist or singer must play or sing the simplest scales every day as exercise, and otherwise will be unable to do anything complicated, as a craftsman needs certain muscular habits, as a wrestler needs training — so in the Christian deed of transfiguring the world a small everyday life should be freely created.

Why speak of the brotherhood of the people, if we do not live with our roommate in brotherly fashion?

Why speak of freedom, if we are unable to freely combine our creative efforts?

Why speak of a Christian attitude toward labor, if we work under the rod or do not work at all?

Free laboring — that is the basis of our path in Christ. And this basis should pervade our everyday and routine life. If it is not so, then the Grand Inquisitor is right, the general party line is right, all the violators, levelers, dictators, and slave-owners are right, and people are not the images of God but a herd.

In this free laboring, our efforts should make of every common deed a sort of monastery, a sort of spiritual organism, a sort of minor order, a sort of brotherhood. If that is not so, it means that we did not understand or accept the most basic thing that there is in the one great monastery, the one great organism, the one order, the one brotherhood that is the Church.

Great is the joy of those who do not doubt that free laboring can be realized in people's lives. And woe to those who shake that faith.

5

Toward a New Monasticism I
At the Heart of the World

In trying to embrace the monastic life, Mother Maria faced the challenge of how to do so in the midst of the Russian emigration. In Paris, her fellow émigrés suffered not only the displacement from their homeland, but the general deprivations of the Great Depression. The would-be monastic shares this common situation — like it or not, he finds himself "not behind strong monastery walls . . . but on all the roads and crossroads of the world, with no opportunity of orienting himself by old traditions, with no hint of new traditions." Here we see Mother Maria coming to terms with a situation in which all the previous "givens" of monastic life have been swept away. Her approach is toward a living tradition, neither the rejection of the past nor the obsessive clinging to the letter of the law, but a practical, authentic effort to locate the tradition in the midst of new circumstances. But she is insistent, as always, that the monk's vocation is not a form of escape from the world but a deep form of service and solidarity.

I cannot feel myself in any way competent to write on monasticism in its essence. That is not what I want to take up as my theme. I would merely like to share some thoughts about the new things now facing monasticism, things that it cannot avoid and, at the same time, that perhaps find little comprehension among secular people.

One often hears mention of "the new monasticism." Some people endow these words with a positive meaning: it's about time, they say. Others think that "new monasticism" means all but "no monasticism," and that there is a lie and a temptation hidden here. And yet I do think that even granted this negative attitude, everyone understands that the new monasticism is something that really exists.

First of all I would like to figure out what this notion means. "New" ... New things can be invented. Life is the same, nothing has changed, the old needs are still there, yet a man, bored with established traditions, tries to change and break up the old, and invents something new. Even in this there is essentially no temptation, because these notions are bound to fail. There is no demand, and nobody needs the supply. The most inveterate, the most hopeless failures take precisely this path. But there are other ways for the "new" to emerge.

For instance, there existed an ancient tradition, based on a Gospel text, of standing in church at the Palm Sunday vigil holding palm branches. This tradition was observed in Byzantium, and that without any difficulty, since it was easy for them to find palm branches. But imagine a Palm Sunday vigil in Moscow or even in Kiev. Where will they get palm branches? The tradition has to be changed. People start cutting pussywillow branches.[18] Probably warily at first, afraid of leading people into temptation — it's a matter of a clear deviation from the Gospel text. Later nothing was left of the temptation, the new thing became a tradition, and so much so that many would probably be tempted now if they were offered fir or birch branches instead of pussywillows. Now there are probably Russian people in Africa, where palm branches are easily obtained, who think: "How's that? 'Pussywillow Sunday' without pussywillows?" In the same way, probably, Byzantine dried figs and olives during the Great Lent were replaced in the Russian north by pickled cabbage. No Greek Typikon[19] makes any mention of this pickled cabbage, but imagine Russian lenten tradition without it! These are all little everyday things, you may say. Let them be little; they show the essence of the matter more easily, because the same things happen on a serious level as well.

There is thus a "new" that is not invented by the idle human mind, but that follows inevitably from the conditions of life. Every attempt to preserve the old on such occasions is either impossible (like palm branches in the north), or does not correspond to the spirit of the old tradition: in Constantinople the simplest food was olives, and so they were prescribed during Lent, while in Moscow an insistence on olives would not be the simplest thing — olives are a rarity there, a delicacy. The simple thing would be cabbage. And only after showing by such insignificant examples how the "new" can be born, should we analyze what we understand by the new contemporary monasticism.

It is undoubtedly not monasticism but only the monastic life that has been going through a crisis for a long time now, perhaps more than a century. In pre-Petrine Russia, in the time of St. Sergius, in the time of Joseph of Volotsk and Nilus of Sora,[20] behind all the varied manifestations of monastic creativity, it was still perfectly clear that life would present this creativity with very specific demands. The supply met a demand. Monastery schools, monastery colonies, monastery farms, monastery publishing houses, monastery educational and cultural centers, and, often, monastery fortresses — and all that was a sure, strong, and steadfast framework for the holiness hidden within them. The cultural and economic traditions of the monasteries are something that cannot be contested. They are simply a historical fact. In Peter's time, with its secularization of life, the demand changed, and so did the supply.

The synodal period of the Church[21] is, of course, a period of the historical decline of monasticism as an idea, as a principle. This does not mean that there were no remarkable monks or remarkable monasteries at that time, but all that was remarkable was rather an exception, it kept failing to discover some strong and general line for the creative monastic path. The old tradition (now corresponding infinitely less to the needs of life) was still being lived out, though no directive for it came from the surrounding life. The synodal period is over, of course. Of the old life, including the monastic life, no stone has been left standing. We may say that today not one old tradition can seek its basis and justification in the conditions of life that brought it into being. Nothing remains of those conditions. A tradition remains, if it does remain, only as such, as a certain petrified rite, whose performers gradually forget the reason for it. Even with the sharpest hatred of novelty and the most ardent striving to preserve the old, it is simply physically impossible to remain outside the new conditions. There are only two possible attitudes toward them, as it actually happens: either to deny the new needs of the time without understanding them — as purposeless, unthinking, unwitting innovations — or, taking this new life into consideration, to innovate according to a plan, in a creative way — more than that, to innovate so as to create a new tradition. In this alone lies the difference between contemporary traditionalists and innovators.

Traditionalists, having no physical possibility of preserving the old, also do not create a new life. Innovators, not trying to preserve the unpreservable, organically create a new life and a new tradition. Thus the roles here are essentially changed.

What are the new conditions of life to which this slowly created future tradition should correspond?

There are, of course, two incommensurable things in the path of contemporary Orthodox monasticism: Soviet life and life abroad. And it may even seem that there is no particular need to say much about life abroad, since in Russia everything is defined by Soviet life and the further self-definition of monasticism will also follow those lines. This last conclusion seems to me totally wrong. Soviet life is not such a permanent quantity that so sensitive and keen a thing as an emerging tradition should orient itself by it. In everything that has any degree of substantiality, it comes very close to the life abroad, as it looks from the monastic point of view. All this evidence can be enumerated. First, there is the absolute homelessness of contemporary monasticism: in Russia the monasteries have been taken away; here they have never existed. The result is an acute orientation toward the world, an immersion in the very depths of the secular element, to the point of earning one's crust of bread among secular people, in the same ways they do. The result of this absence of normal monastic life is a certain impression of archaism, of unattachment, almost of untimeliness of contemporary monasticism in the world. We can put it like this: innovation is determined by the fact that the modern monk, *whether he likes it or not,* finds himself not behind strong monastery walls, within defined, ossified traditions, but on all the roads and crossroads of the world, with no opportunity of orienting himself by old traditions, with no hint of new traditions. And woe to him who dislikes these worldly roads and crossroads: he will neither preserve the old, nor create the new. In other words: today's monasticism must fight for its very core, for its very soul, disregarding all external forms, creating new forms.

Let us imagine a person who not only strives toward the core, toward the soul of monasticism, but who also does not want to embody his monasticism in the forms of the old tradition. Oh, he knows very well how the brothers used to save their souls, how there used to be sketes,[22] how they lived in seclusion — he knows all that and he does not want any of it. He is tonsured a monk. In most cases he is also ordained a priest. There is no monastery, no skete, no seclusion. Instead, there are the wide roads of life, a parish, maybe even in some backwater, and in the parish all the pains, all the wounds, all the sins of life, with drunkenness, depravity, thoughts of suicide. And, on the other hand, there is the longing for a little material well-being, there is competition, there is peaceful and quiet "everyday" godlessness — all that he saw in the world and that he wanted to leave behind, and did not leave behind, because he had *nowhere to go.* Nowhere, because as a monk he is not needed, or perhaps monasticism is not needed?

Absolutely wrong. He is both needed and not needed, precisely he, as a monk, because monasticism in general is needed, but it is needed mainly on the roads of life, in the very thick of it. Today there is only one monastery for a monk — the whole world. This he must inevitably understand very soon, and in this lies the force of his *innovation.* Here many must become innovators against their will. This is the meaning, the cause, and the justification of the new monasticism!

The new here is not characterized mainly by its newness, but by its being *inevitable*. There is no need to seek in these statements for any non-recognition of the old form of monasticism on principle. But, needed as it is, it does not exhaust what the churchly world now has the right to expect from monasticism. It may be only a part, and, owing to external circumstances, an insignificant part, of contemporary monasticism.

Imagine a monk faced with the possibility of choosing: monastery or world. Let us suppose that his character and his notion of monasticism are such that he wants the monastery. Isn't that too much to want? It would be normal for the whole world to want to be in a monastery, but the whole world does not have access to an external monastery! A gravely ill person wants a sanatorium, mountain air, fortifying nourishment, medical help — but not every sick person has access to it. Many must of necessity content themselves with a dark little basement, poor food, bad air. The same thing happens in the spiritual world. A monastery is like a spiritual sanatorium: we do not all have an incontestable right to it. There is more love, more humility, more need in remaining in the world's backyard, in breathing its bad air, in hungering after spiritual food — sharing all these burdens and all the world's anguish with others, lightening them for others.

Christ, in ascending to heaven, did not take the Church with Him; He did not halt the path of human history. Christ left the Church in the world. It was left as a small bit of leavening, but this leavening is to leaven the whole lump (Gal 5:9). In other words, within the limits of history, Christ gave the whole world to the Church, and she has no right to renounce its spiritual edification and transfiguration. And for that she needs a strong army. That army is monasticism.

6

Toward a New Monasticism II
Love without Limits

The three vows of monastic profession are examined: obedience, chastity, and poverty (nonpossession). Mother Maria finds concrete expression for each, not only within monastery walls but also in loving service to the suffering neighbors around us. She points to a truly Gospel-based monasticism, precisely what the earliest monastics, the fathers and mothers of the desert, put into practice. In the face of the neighbor, one sees the face of God.

It would be absurd and senseless to try to create monasteries now as they used to be before the revolution, to continue old traditions at all costs and sacrifice our whole life to them. With regard to monasticism this is the more clear, as it is essentially impossible to say which tradition should be taken up and restored. The eighteenth and nineteenth centuries were generally periods of decadence in the history of monasticism, and they can hardly be adopted without introducing very essential corrections from more remote times.

What, in fact, was monasticism in this latest period of its existence? It is customary to think that the most widespread type in Russia was the type of the contemplative monk, and that Orthodox monasticism, in contrast to Roman Catholic, renounced all external activity in the name of solitary relations with God.

I think that this is totally wrong. There were contemplatives, but there were only a few thousand of them, personally called to such endeavor. They may have represented the high point of monastic life, but they by no means determined the basic type. Of course, it is unquestionably true that Russian monasticism, with very few exceptions, did not have any active social tasks in the church life of the last few centuries. But this negative feature does not turn it into contemplative monasticism. To understand what it used to be, we need only study what remains of it in Romania, Latvia, Estonia, and elsewhere. A monastery used to be a family hearth, as it were, with the monastic community replacing the family. Brothers and sisters replaced parents and children. This monastic family was a sort of economic and domestic unity, and — what was most characteristic of it — it was a religious laboring community that ministered to both the spiritual and material interests of its members. People from the outside world also flowed to this center. They, of course, derived a certain material and spiritual satisfaction from it as well, but that was a secondary matter for the monastery — coming from an overflow of its forces, so to speak, not from its main purpose.

There is nothing bad about such an understanding of tasks. It is very possible that historical circumstances forced the monks to limit them in that way. But it would be totally incorrect to recognize this limitation as something unique and obligatory. It would be incorrect to think that monasticism cannot exist outside this historical framework, and that we are now called at all costs to recreate what existed earlier — and, if the life conditions for it are not there, to create at least an external stage set, to restore the historically accurate costumes, so to speak, of the old monasticism.

To give a correct answer to the question of what the paths of contemporary monasticism are, we must, of course, examine not only what they were in the nineteenth century or in still older centuries, but also what are the most essential, mystical, and profound features of Orthodox monasticism, its innermost essence, its basic principles.

Monasticism is determined not by a way of life, not by the monastery, not by the desert; monasticism is determined by the vows made during the rite of tonsuring. The rest is a historical covering, which can and must change, and which has only relative value: it is valuable as long as it contributes to the fulfillment of the vows.

These vows are three: obedience, chastity, and nonpossession. If a monk keeps them, he keeps monasticism; if he breaks them, then despite all his monastic life he has not kept his monasticism.

The vow of chastity has always been understood with perfect clarity, and historical conditions, of course, cannot introduce any changes in it. Therefore the root of the "new" that monasticism should adopt is not to be found there.

The other two vows developed in opposite directions over the last two centuries. All the emphasis was placed on the vow of obedience, and the principle of the cutting off of all will was brought to its ultimate limit. The vow of nonpossession, meanwhile, was simplified to an elementary renunciation of the love of money or, at best, of one's own material property. It was given no more spiritual interpretation.

This special emphasis on the vow of obedience can be explained by the strong development of the institution of *starchestvo*,[23] which we observe in Russian monasticism from the end of the eighteenth century. *Starchestvo* is the close spiritual guidance of the monk, implying the total surrender of his will into the hands of the *starets*. It is not only a question of the discipline necessary in any communal life, not only a question of following the rules of this communal life, not only a question of voluntarily taking upon oneself certain duties and the responsibility for their fulfillment. On the contrary, under obedience responsibility is removed, as it were, and duties are not the consequence of their place in the communal life, but of a blind and unquestioning fulfillment of the will of the *starets*. One thing is required of the monk: not only that he have no will of his own, but that he have no reasoning, no evaluation, no choice of his own. The *starets* evaluates, chooses, reasons, and decides for him; the monk is only the blind executor of these decisions. The following example may be cited as the limit of such obedience: if the *starets* falls into heresy and is exposed, the monk continues to obey him, because

by disobeying he would sin, he would break the vow of obedience, while by fulfilling the heretical demands of the *starets* he
does not sin, because the very fact of obedience shifts all responsibility for the sin onto the one who is guiding the monk's life,
that is, the *starets*.

There is no need for me to consider the essence of this principle right now. The important thing is to underscore that its
realization sets one necessary condition: for obedience one needs
a *starets* who must be obeyed. If there is no *starets*, there is no
obedience, or, in any case, it changes its character, it becomes relative, conditional. A *starets* is not merely some chance superior,
he is a man who responsibly takes another's fate in his hands,
watches over it daily and attentively, educates his disciple, answers for him before God. If a *starets* is a true spiritual father for
a disciple, the disciple, too, should be a true, well-guided, beloved
son for the *starets*. Without that there can be no *starchestvo* and
no obedience.

And we must say firmly that, in the contemporary conditions
of monastic life, there is no *starchestvo* or almost none. And that
is natural. In the Russia of that time, with its many thousands
of monks, there were always a few people capable of being real
startsy, and their fame spread all over the country, while with
us, here abroad, we have to seek for *startsy* among a few dozen
monks. The choice is therefore reduced to the utmost limits.
There are, of course, spiritually experienced monks of the most
lofty life among us, but in most cases they are overloaded with
a variety of church affairs of a managerial and administrative as
well as a purely religious nature. They are physically unable to
follow attentively the spiritual life of their disciples, the more so
as these disciples often not only do not live in the same monastery, or in the same town, but not even in the same country. This
fact alone is enough to explain what *starchestvo* has become in
our conditions. Any monk who happens to have been ordained
several years ago can now become a *starets*. His conscience tells
him of his inexperience, and that is why he does not present his
disciple with any particular demands, but limits his role to being
useful to him as far as he can.

Along with that, life itself confronts monks with the most diverse decisions, and demands responsibility from them almost from the very first day after their tonsuring. They find themselves virtually on their own, if not simply abandoned. In such conditions, it would be absurd to try at all costs to restore the institution of *starchestvo*, to consider one person conventionally a *starets* and another a disciple, to apply the whole strict system of obedience as a total cutting off of the will in order to be given into the hands of another person.

Obedience as such remains unchanged, but its meaning becomes different. A monk should be obedient to the work of the Church to which he is assigned; he should give his will and all his creative powers entirely to this work. Obedience becomes service. In essence, this service should be no less strict than obedience to a *starets*. Only here responsibility rests with the monk himself, he himself takes the measure of his conscientiousness, his sacrificial self-giving. The Church herself becomes his *starets*, and also judges him, while the obedience requested is the responsible fulfillment of what the Church has charged him to do.

Is this an innovation? Perhaps so, but here life itself is the innovator. It does not ask us whether we want to understand the vow of obedience we have made in this or some other way. It tells us that in contemporary conditions it cannot be understood in any other way. Our business is only to understand its demands and to name them accurately. Of course, some sort of artificial reconstruction of the old understanding is possible, with some sort of conventional distribution of the roles of *startsy* and disciples, but that very artificiality and conventionality speak against such attempts, and life does nothing but destroy such unions, scattering people to different countries, burdening them with personal responsibility for the personal business required of them.

The question here is simple: we need not to restore the old but to try responsibly to accept the new, to comprehend it, to make out precisely what it demands of us.

And, finally, the third vow: nonpossession. It is only at first sight that the vow of nonpossession seems to have been reduced and simplified; in fact, that is not so; what is so is rather the opposite — the vow of nonpossession is in need of greater comprehension and deepening.

Today, in secular life, the actual love of money is something extremely unreal. Everyone works in order to be able to feed himself and his family, and dreams of nothing more. Here a nonpossessing monk will be one of the countless nonpossessing people around him. We all know very well the worthlessness of material well-being; we have simply lost the habit of it. An ordinary émigré is essentially more of a nonpossessor than an ordinary monk of older times. Such are the conditions of life.

Private property. A great many people would willingly renounce it in exchange for the right to use common property that would afford them a roof, clothing, and food. Here everything is relative.

But there are things in the idea of nonpossession that are not relative, and that are especially obvious now. It cannot be limited to a material understanding. A destitute and non-money-loving man can at the same time be a great spiritual possessor.

What are the fundamental texts on which the idea of nonpossession is based? It seems to me that they are the commandment about the blessedness of the poor in spirit, for theirs is the Kingdom of Heaven, and the affirmation that no one has any greater love than to give his soul for his friends. If that is so, then what is particularly contrary to nonpossession? We see a special meaning in the answer to this question, because from it follow the great actuality, the great urgency and timeliness of the principle of nonpossession. What is particularly contrary to it is egocentrism, the disease of our time.

Egocentrism defines itself not so much by material miserliness and greed as by their spiritual manifestations. The egocentric accumulates spiritual riches and is greedy for them. He opposes himself to the world. The world comes out as some sort of background for his development, some sort of favorable or unfavorable milieu that has no meaning or significance of its own. Yet it is not some sort of abstract world but the concrete world that surrounds him. The whole lexicon of the egocentric is sprinkled with the words "I" and "mine." "His" friend is someone whom he needs and whom he wants to make use of. "His" family is his property, which must provide comfort and deliver him from solitude, without imposing any particular responsibility on him. His science, his art, his motherland — these are all dear and necessary notions that contribute to his spiritual and material soundness and weightiness. He is the center for which creation exists. Divine justice and divine mercy are measured from the point of view of his needs. If he does good deeds, it is in order to exercise his virtue in them. Any number of examples can be given here. We may say that any relationship, external or internal, material or spiritual, can always be an expression of egocentrism — religious life is also not free of it. And in exactly the same way, the principle of nonpossession can be expressed in any relationship. The subtler the egocentrism, the higher the limits of the human spirit it reaches, the more repulsive it is. The subtler the nonpossession, the greater the spiritual values a person renounces, the more fully he gives his soul for his friends, the holier he is, and the more he corresponds to what Christ demands of him.

Of course, a monk who makes a vow should strive to fulfill it in the most absolute and all-embracing sense. In the sphere of external things, a monk should first of all be non-money-loving and a man who owns no private property, or if he does, he should place no value on it. A monk should not be attached to anything for its own sake, because he finds it useful, or pleasing, or comforting, or edifying. His relation to everything should be determined by the possibility of giving himself, sacrificing himself, being crucified for the other. His own salvation and the striving for it he should submit totally to the words of the apostle Paul: "I could wish to be separated from Christ, in order to see my brothers saved" (cf. Rom 9:3). Essentially, this is a paraphrase of Christ's words about giving one's soul for one's friends.

Poverty of spirit is not, of course, the renunciation of any intellectual interests; it is not a sort of spiritual idiocy. It is the renunciation of one's spiritual exclusiveness, it is the giving of one's spirit to the service of God's work on earth, and it is the only path for common life in the one *sobornoe*[24] organism of the Church.

A monk should find the strength in himself to say together with Christ: "Into thy hands I commend my spirit" (Lk 23:46). He should consciously want to become the fulfiller of God's work on earth — and nothing else. He should be a conductor of divine love and a co-participant in divine sacrifice.

And it is completely false and incorrect to think that he should constantly protect some inner cell, some Holy of Holies of his own, to give without giving the main thing. He should first of all sacrificially give the main thing, remembering that the Founder of his endeavor, the Savior Himself, lifted up on the cross all His divinity and all His humanity, that in His sacrifice He gave up all of Himself, and that is precisely what He expects of those who follow in his footsteps.

Nonpossession should not be merely passive — they don't ask, so I don't give. Nonpossession should be active: a monk should seek where to place the gifts given him by God precisely for that end.

It goes without saying that this point of view implies the necessity of monastic activity in the outside world. But it should be remembered that all its forms — social work, charity, spiritual aid — are the result of an intense desire to give one's strength to the activity of Christ, to the humanity of Christ, not to possess but to spend it for the glory of God.

It seems to me that this new understanding of the vow of nonpossession should determine the path of the modern monk. In practice, he may acquire some new and unaccustomed appearance because of it, but that is an external thing. In reality, he will stand on the foundation of the ancient vows that determine the very essence of his monastic effort.

7

The Poor in Spirit

In this short text, Mother Maria reflects further on poverty's most constructive, affirmative expression, limitless love for the neighbor, a reflection of God's emptying Himself for us in limitless love.

For many people the promise of blessedness for the poor in spirit seems incomprehensible. What they find incomprehensible are the implications of the phrase "poverty of spirit." Certain fanatics think it means the impoverishment of the spirit, its deliverance from all thinking; they come close to affirming the sinfulness of all thinking, of all intellectual life. Others, who refuse to accept such an explanation, are prepared to consider the word "spirit" little short of an interpolation into the authentic Gospel text.

Let us figure out how we must understand this expression.

In the rite of monastic tonsuring, among other vows, the tonsured person makes a vow of nonpossession, that is, of poverty, which can be understood in a materialist way as a renunciation of the accumulation of material riches. The strict fulfillment of this vow would lead to the blessedness of the poor, but such a narrow and materialist interpretation does not uncover the whole meaning of the phrase: "blessed are the poor in spirit."

The vow of nonpossession can and should be expanded to the spiritual domain; the person who makes it should also renounce spiritual possession, which brings him to the spiritual poverty for which blessedness is promised. But what is spiritual nonpossession?

Nonpossession in general is opposed to two vices between which we make little distinction in our everyday life: the vice of miserliness and the vice of greed. Analyzing them, we will see that a miserly person may not be greedy at all, while a greedy one may even be a spendthrift. It is possible to imagine these two vices in the form of a formula like this. The miserly person says: "What's mine is mine," but does not always add: "What's yours is also mine." The greedy person says: "What's yours is mine," but, again, does not always add: "What's mine is also mine." He may be especially anxious to possess what is not his, while not being very careful about what he has. There exists, of course, a level at which greed combines with miserliness, and vice versa. This is when one says: "What's mine is mine, and what's yours is also mine."

A nonpossessing person should be free of both miserliness and greed; he should say: "What's mine is yours, and what's yours is also yours." And it would be too simple to think that this concerns only material goods. Nonpossession, the absence of miserliness and greed, should concern a person's entire inner world. We know that Christ taught us to lay down our soul for our friends. This laying down of the soul, this giving of oneself, is what makes a person poor in spirit. It is the opposite in everyday life; even with the most negative attitude toward material possession, we are used to regarding the spiritual holding back of ourselves as something positive. Whereas it is the most terrible sin, because it is not material but spiritual.

Thus the virtue of nonpossession, spiritually understood, should make a person open to the world and to people. Life outside the Church, and in part a distorted understanding of Christianity, accustom us to hoarding our inner riches, to being eternally curious — that is, greedy with regard to our neighbor's spiritual world. We often hear it said that man should know measure in his love, should limit himself, and that this measure is his self-preservation, his spiritual well-being, his way of salvation.

Christ did not know measure in His love for people. And in this love He reduced His Divinity to the point of incarnation

and took upon Himself the suffering of the universe. In this sense
His example teaches us not measure in love but the absolute and
boundless giving of ourselves, determined by the laying down of
our soul for our friends.

Without striving for such giving of oneself, there is no following the path of Christ.

And it is not Christ but the non-Christian ideal that speaks
to us of the hoarding of inner and outer riches. We know what
this ideal leads to, we know the egoism and egocentrism that
reign in the world, we know how people are turned in upon
themselves, upon their own well-being, their peace of mind, their
various interests. And we know more. People's care for their spiritual peace, their locking themselves away, leads before our eyes
to self-poisoning, demoralization, loss of joy; they become un-
bearable to themselves, turn neurasthenic. In a most paradoxical
way, they become poor from holding on to themselves, because
their eternal self-attention and self-admiration transform them.
The poor hold on to their rags and do not know that the only
way not only to preserve them but also to make them precious is
to give them with joy and love to those who need them.

And why?

These rags are the corruptible riches of the kingdom of this
world. By giving them away, by giving himself away entirely, with
his whole inner world, laying down his soul, a man becomes
poor in spirit, one of the blessed, because his is the Kingdom
of Heaven, according to our Savior's promise, because he becomes the owner of the incorruptible and eternal riches of that
Kingdom, becomes it at once, here on earth, acquiring the joy
of unmeasured, self-giving, and sacrificial love, the lightness and
freedom of nonpossession.

8

Under the Sign of Our Time

Herself a refugee from the Russian Revolution, Mother Maria was intimately familiar with the pains of exile. But here she examines this experience under a positive light, reflecting on the mysterious "blessings" of being uprooted and deprived of the familiar and secure life of one's homeland. What applies to all emigrants, applies as well to the Orthodox Church. Here too in exile a great gift and challenge has been given to the Church — the freedom to return to the sources, the essentials of the Gospel.

When people live in their native land, when they are citizens or subjects of some state, then, though they may be extremely opposed to its principles, they continue to be answerable to it. To have some faith, some conviction, some opinion, while being within a certain state system, means to bear the consequences of that opinion and conviction. If it coincides with the opinion of the authorities, the man achieves general recognition, the opportunity to realize himself, to show himself, to attain wealth, position, and so on. If the opinion differs from the opinion of the majority, then the man must bear the responsibility for it, he is persecuted, deprived of freedom, his life is broken, he can even be destroyed — executed, worn out in exile, and so on.

Such is the life of all who have not left their motherland, who are bound up with its historical destiny. And whether that motherland is Russia, Germany, Spain, or even France — every citizen in it knows what he can be punished for, what those punishments will be, and what will bring him universal success and recognition. And that concerns not only those of his views that are connected with the political regime of the given country, but also his faith, his worldview. The worldview becomes responsible. Faith may be confessed under the condition of a readiness for martyrdom. Everything acquires significance, everything determines the necessity of a clear-cut and decisive choice. And, along with that, an enormous, an almost insuperable pressure bears upon the possibility of that choice. If I have only a vague sympathy for a certain opinion, then, faced with all the possible punishments for that opinion, I am going to think again whether it is worth confessing it quite openly. And only if I am absolutely and irretrievably caught up by certain convictions will I dare go all the way in defending them — to torture and even to death.

The result is a certain caution in the souls of those who are connected with their national organism, the great influence of this organism on each of its members, constraint, dependence. I do not know if it is worthwhile giving examples — there is an infinite number of them. If one risks going to Solovki[25] for participating in a procession with the cross, then a man, perhaps even a staunch one, may refrain from participating in it — simply so as not to expend his whole life for a procession with the cross, but to save it for a more purposeful martyrdom. Any choice confronts "citizens" as a sort of final line, beyond which they begin to bear responsibility with their entire life. And, at the same time, a "citizen" is always unfree, always feels the whole weight of oppressive power upon him, of public opinion, tradition, everyday life, the history of his country. We know all this, because it all took place in our own lives. We know that in the time of the Russian civil war, choice implied death, imprisonment, exile, the total crippling of one's life. We remember what it meant to bear the responsibility for one's views; we remember the absence of freedom in confessing them. And still more we know what it means to confess one's faith where it is persecuted, where the whole force of the state is raised against it. We know how people would be deprived of their crust of bread for the baptismal cross on their neck, how they would be sent to the camps for a book of religious content, and so on.

Now we've become émigrés. What does that mean? First of all it means freedom. It means a sort of absolute falling out of the rule of law, a sort of ultimate deliverance from all external responsibility, an extremely painful and at the same time blissful sense of being beyond the influence of power, public opinion, tradition, everyday life, and the history of our country. It is as though we have lost our weightiness, lost our corporeality, acquired an enormous mobility and lightness, become unbound. And we are not answerable to anyone for anything. If we have faith, nobody cares about it. If we hold certain extreme opinions in the political sphere, they have no effect: we cannot, even by participating passively in elections, give an extra vote to the man we sympathize with. We are almost like shadows. Our own public opinion has no force. Perhaps no one is ever so much outside the whole process of life as the person who has lost all his civil rights and responsibilities, as the person who has become so fully irresponsible, as the émigré. The "citizen" has the opportunity of realizing himself, bearing the incredible overhead expenses of this realization; he must constantly overcome the friction of his milieu, of public opinion, of tradition. We do not have to overcome any friction, we do not have any overhead expenses, but we are almost deprived of the possibility of realizing ourselves, because we are deprived of corporeality, we have no point on which to apply our forces.

Such is the objective character of our condition. But apart from the necessity of characterizing it, we have the need to comprehend it religiously. At the beginning of the nineteenth century there existed a whole pleiad of social utopians who dreamed of creating a new life on uninhabited islands, built on new and just laws coming from outside the old and unjust tradition. They did not succeed in finding any uninhabited islands. These uninhabited islands have been given to us without our will in the very centers of world history. We have to set up our monarchies or republics, our communities, our hermitages, in Paris or New York. The owner of the neighborhood bistro could not care less what

regime we have, whether we believe in God or worship proto-
plasm. The prefecture demands of us some minimal order in our
passports, the tax inspector collects our taxes — those are our
only ties with the external world. And our internal émigré world
is too strengthless and bodiless to actively show its displeasure by
this or that trend in its own milieu.

What, then, does our special, abnormal life call us to? What
has this total absence of inertia, this disincarnation, this boundless freedom from all external coercion already brought us to?
In what measure have we proved worthy of it? In what measure
have we realized it creatively?

We, the children of war and revolution, we who know the
power and law of catastrophe, ruin, and death, we who have acquired a terrible wisdom in the period of our collapse, we who
know the fragility of all well-being and the illusiveness of all
stability — we find ourselves once more in a contemporary un-
stable world, which is awaiting new catastrophes, raving with
coming wars, torn by civil war, awaiting unprecedented historical
cataclysms. It would seem that our bitter experience should have
made us more keen sighted, more wise. We should have been able
to place a true value on the blessings of life, on its durability. In
fact, we have all submitted in varying degrees to the opinions that
exist in the surrounding milieu. If we think better and look at it
attentively, we are struck most of all by a sort of psychological
stolidity, carelessness, mediocrity, an absence of any real uneasi-
ness in it, an affirmation of petty everyday life on the side of a
volcano that is about to become active. . . . In our very unhappiness, we feel quite happy, we build nests on a cliff that is bound to
collapse, we submit to spiritual philistinism, spiritual mediocrity,
lukewarmness. This concerns everyone. Everyone nowadays lacks
true religious fire; everything around us smolders and smokes.

If we turn our attention to our Church milieu, to those in
whose life the Church occupies a large place, who define themselves in terms of their Orthodoxy, we must confess that our
observations will not be especially joyful. Of course, there are
always righteous people in the Church — we have them, too.
There are always pure and unworldly souls in the Church — and

we can meet them now as well. But apart from that, there is a vast group of people in the Church who understand Orthodoxy as some attribute of their belonging to the old Russian state, as some sort of non-existent life, as a testimony of political loyalty and political rightmindedness. To a certain degree this becomes our Church's public opinion, issuing a patent for what is allowed and what is forbidden, seeking out heretics, dreaming of the time when the secular power, with the entire force of its punitive and police apparatus, will preserve the purity of Orthodoxy, while the Church will condemn anti-government tendencies with its spiritual authority.

There is another pole of attraction for other forces in our Church life. It is also to be found in a newly formed group — the so-called patriarchal church — perhaps more refined and cultured than the first. What they have in common is a fear of living relations with life, a worship of the letter, an elevation of canons to the level of the divinely revealed truth, a belief in the infallibility of the conventional, a desire to seek out and denounce heresies. But this second group, perhaps owing to the higher intellectual level of its members, shows a stronger aesthetic intuition, the principle of a sort of historical rapture over churchly beauty. Besides that, while the first Church group is thoroughly poisoned by politics, the second is rather diverse and imprecise in the political respect. It is also conservative, also watches over the foundations, but these foundations are somewhat different than in the first group: it is not going to resurrect the synodal period of the Church,[26] it strives for things that are more beautiful and archaic. Any allusion to freedom is foreign to it. If it were to refuse state measures of enforcement to bring dissenters to reason, it would do so only because it relies on a different way of bringing people to reason — with the fires of the inquisition set up by the Church herself. It has a strain of fanaticism in it, it also has a certain creativity, but this creativity is blind to our contemporary life, it is a sort of scheming, loveless creativity.

If the question were exhausted by the presence of these strata of the emigration alone, then generally there could be no two opinions about its fate. It would mean that the entire mass of

Russian people who find themselves torn away from their native soil is not strong enough to bear the heavy burden of freedom and the absence of responsibility. Freedom has burned them. The desert turned out to be peopled by a dark force, and the dark force has swallowed them. But is there something else in the emigration, and what should this something else be? What would it have to be, for the emigration to have inner, spiritual meaning, to justify itself?

I will not affirm or deny the existence of this last group. I will limit myself only to characterizing what it would have to be, though I think that if it did not exist, we would have long since lost the ability to breathe.

First of all, we should understand the providential meaning of the freedom given us. We must receive it as a weighty gift, and not only relate to it externally, but let it penetrate to the very depths of our spirit, rethink and test in its light all our usual and habitual opinions and bases. If we are free of the influence of the state and power, are we sufficiently liberated from the canon of convictions, customs, and rules that we ourselves create? From his earliest youth a man gradually includes in a sort of inner reference book whole chapters and pages of other people's opinions. Having once received them ardently and vividly, he then introduces them into a sort of obligatory list of what is appropriate. These opinions go dead, they no longer correspond to the present state of his soul but to something long past. Yet he repeats them year after year, because he lacks courage or time to revise, as it were, the inventory of his worldview. He continues to act not according to his inner need, but according to his unquestioning trust in his own past worldview. Everything is so well set up, so habitual, has acquired such solid, even aesthetic, forms, that oftentimes one cannot even lift a finger to disturb this settled picture of inner peace. We are tightly buttoned up in our worldview, we are well-dressed, we are simply swaddled in it.

And we are rightly afraid to find ourselves in a state of freedom in this domain. For it may be the only stable thing we have left. And it must take some inner catastrophe, some ultimate and profound impoverishment, some striving for the most ruthless honesty, to make a man venture to put everything into doubt, to renounce all opportunity of speaking in the name of Dosto-evsky, or Khomiakov, or Soloviev,[27] and begin to speak only in the name of his own conscience, of this or that degree of his love and his knowledge of God. But hard as it is to say to im-poverished people: "Become still more impoverished" — that is the inner command of the freedom given to us. Everything seems small and accidental in its light except the most terrible questions of life and death, God's love and God's interference in our des-tiny. This is the first and main thing: not to allow cowardliness or the comfort of a certain kind of aesthetic worldview to ob-scure our terrible standing in the desert before God. In this sense we must also emigrate out of this well-being, we must open our souls to all the drafts and winds of absolute inner freedom. Such, it seems to me, are our inner paths.

Going on to their external manifestation and realization, we must first of all understand the mysterious meaning of the fact that, while we have lost our earthly motherland, we have not lost our heavenly motherland, that the Church is with us, in our midst — the whole Orthodox Church in her entirety, not divided into any sub-churches. She is whole in Russia, and she is whole in the emigration, and she is whole in every parish. And this is the only place where we can still realize ourselves, and the only work which, despite all, can succeed.

Let us look at the Church's work from the point of view of our freedom, which obligates us here as nowhere else. First I want to make one reservation. Not long ago I happened to speak on this subject in a certain magazine. My article provoked a response that came as a total surprise to me. The mere observation of the fact of our extraordinary freedom, compared with the situation of the Church in all the time of her existence, made certain people suppose for some reason that I consider only the life of our émigré Church authentic, and that I throw away, cross out, count as nothing the two thousand years of Church history. Beyond that, the conclusion was drawn that I deny the righteousness and holiness of the Church in the time of her state captivity. It is hard to refute such arbitrary and totally unfounded conclusions drawn from one's own precise words. Perhaps the thing to do is not refute them, but simply repeat the same thoughts in different words until they finally become comprehensible. The history of the Church in all times contains pages devoted to authentic holiness. Privation of freedom in no case diminishes the possibility of holiness; what's more, it may be precisely in periods of the maximum privation of freedom that the most obvious, most unquestionable holiness blossoms. So it is in times of persecution, which are also times of martyrdom. I think, too, that the heavy pressure of state violence in periods of protection by state power, while crushing the religious will of some, has made others into authentic confessors of Christ's truth.

But the Church's destiny need not only be considered from the point of view of the increase of holiness. Any point of view, the singling out of any sphere of the Church's life and the clarifying of any form of the Church's creativity, is equally legitimate. One can speak about the Church from the point of view of Church art, of the development of dogma, of the transformation of Church administration, etc. And so it is quite as legitimate to speak about the Church's life from the point of view of her freedom. And no one who says that the Church was not free is thereby saying that there was no holiness in her, or that she was torn apart by heresies, or anything else except one thing — that she was not free. And in asserting our freedom, we are asserting only this one fact — that the émigré Church is free. And from this fact our conscience makes us draw particular conclusions. Because our conscience must feel itself responsible for that freedom, must justify itself, must honestly receive this great and weighty gift.

Freedom obliges, freedom calls for sacrificial self-giving, freedom determines one's honesty and strictness with oneself and one's path. And if we want to be strict and honest, worthy of the freedom given us, we must first of all test our own attitude toward our spiritual world. We have no right to wax tenderhearted over all our past indiscriminately — much of that past is far loftier and purer than we are, but much of it is sinful and criminal. We should aspire to the lofty and combat the sinful.

We cannot stylize everything as some sweet ringing of Moscow bells — religion dies of stylization. We cannot cultivate dead customs — only authentic spiritual fire has weight in religious life. We cannot freeze a living soul with rules and orders — once, in their own time, they were the expression of other living souls, but new souls demand a corresponding expression. We cannot see the Church as a sort of aesthetic perfection and limit ourselves to aesthetic swooning — our God-given freedom calls us to activity and struggle. And it would be a great lie to tell searching souls: "Go to church, because there you will find peace." The opposite is true. She tells those who are at peace and asleep: "Go to church, because there you will feel real alarm about your sins, about your perdition, about the world's sins and perdition. There you will feel an unappeasable hunger for Christ's truth. There instead of lukewarm you will become ardent, instead of pacified you will become alarmed, instead of learning the wisdom of this world you will become foolish in Christ."

It is to this foolishness, this folly in Christ, that our freedom calls us. Freedom calls us, contrary to the whole world, contrary not only to the pagans but to many who style themselves Christians, to undertake the Church's work in what is precisely the most difficult way.

And we will become fools in Christ, because we know not only the difficulty of this path but also the immense happiness of feeling God's hand upon what we do.

9

A Justification of Pharisaism

In the New Testament, the Pharisees do not receive good press. Yet Mother Maria gives them credit for an important function. The "pharisee" — a type that appears all throughout religious history, into our own time — preserves the tradition in desperate times. "They do actually and authentically watch over, keep, preserve, and bear the coffer of Christian treasures through the narrow passes of dead and self-satisfied eras." But their value depends on the era in which they live. Now at the dawn of a new era, the pharisees are those who try to protect the Church against authentic Christian fervor, "against all fire in general." In the face of this pharisaic impulse, Mother Maria asks how the fire of the faith, the breath of the Spirit can be allowed to bring life to us today.

The Gospel narrative has engraved in it, as in a small crystal, all that happens and all that can happen in the world. In this sense, world history is a sort of macrocosm in which the same forces are at work as in the Gospel.

It is not enough to say only that the events of the Savior's life are accomplished in the world eternally, that Christ is born into the world and the Child lies in the manger in Bethlehem eternally, that His preaching is heard and His miracles are accomplished eternally; it is not enough to feel that the cross of Golgotha is eternally raised over the world and that the Truth is eternally crucified on it. It is not enough to behold the eternal Resurrection, the eternal Truth abiding in the world; and even the sense of apocalyptic fulfillments, not only threatening the world but also being eternally realized in human history, does not exhaust that which eternally becomes incarnate in the world.

In a certain sense, each human soul shown and revealed to us in the Gospel is reflected in the course of human history. The fallen woman continues to wash the Savior's feet with her tears in the same way, the herd of swine throws itself into the deeps in the same way, the publican is converted in the same way, and in the same way the disciples leave their nets to follow Christ. Peter eternally denies Christ and, through faith, eternally walks on the water; Christ is eternally opposed by doctors of the law, scribes, and pharisees, who ask Him devious questions and betray Him, and the crowd shouts: "Crucify Him, crucify Him!"

In the macrocosm of the universe, in world history, we recognize whole periods that stand under one or another sign of the Gospel narrative. There is, of course, no Gospel chronology, because within God's providence our temporary earthly sequence is accidental. Perhaps the whole series of Gospel events exists all the time, the Nativity simultaneously with Golgotha, and Golgotha with the Resurrection.

We simply feel that each epoch mainly brings forth what is closest and most peculiar to itself.

Long ages go by when the scribes, doctors of the law, and pharisees safeguard the law bequeathed them by their fathers, when everything is calm in this eternal, universal Israel, the prophets are silent, sacrifices are offered in the temple, the pharisee beats his breast and thanks God that he is not like this publican. Then fire breaks out in the world. Again and again comes the Forerunner's call to repentance, again and again settled life is broken up, and the fishermen abandon their nets, and people leave their dead unburied to follow Him. And the eternal prophecy is fulfilled: the house is left empty, the sun goes out, the earth is shattered — and man has no refuge.

Golgotha grows, becomes the whole world. There is nothing left but the Cross.

Mankind is called to sacrifice. And falling, betraying, breaking down, rising again, it goes to this sacrifice. There is no need to draw precise historical parallels. It goes without saying that we cannot achieve a portrait likeness, but at the same time it is clear to everyone what sort of epoch we live in.

Each of us remembers how, still recently, the pharisee's prayers of thanksgiving rang out in a well-fed and stable world, and each of us now hears the crowd shouting outside the windows: "Crucify Him, crucify Him!"

And each of us feels the heavy tread of Him who carries His cross up to Golgotha.

Besides such an eternal macrocosmic incarnation of the Gospel in the world, there is something else, there exists a microcosm of the Gospel narrative — this is each separate human soul. And it is not as though each person is given one of the Gospel images to repeat. No, each of us repeats the entire Gospel, or, rather, can repeat the entire Gospel.

We combine in ourselves both the publican and the pharisee; we pray simultaneously, "I believe, Lord, help my unbelief," and we all believe and believe, and we follow after Christ, and we betray Him, and we hang next to Him on the cross and, like the thief, call out to Him to remember us in His Kingdom. In this sense the promise Christ gave to the sinful woman is true, that what she had done for Him would be remembered wherever the Gospel is proclaimed.

And we may speak not only of the imitation of Christ, but also of a sort of inevitable imitation of the Gospel; not only of man's striving toward the perfection of Christ, but also of his falling into all the abysses the Gospel tells us of.

Man is in eternal discord, in schism, in ceaseless argument with himself. And his inner path is, on the one hand, determined by his own laws, by inexpressible inner events, by changes in the mysterious landscapes of his soul, and, on the other hand, is dependent on the inner path of the epoch in which he lives, reflects it, collaborates with it.

If the epoch is pharisaic, it is very hard for a man not to be a pharisee; if the epoch is imbued with tragedy, if everything around him is perishing, if mankind feels itself on Golgotha — then the individual man accepts this tragedy of life much more easily, walks more easily along the path of sacrifice, consciously taking the cross on his shoulders.

In this sense the macrocosm is connected with the microcosm. They are mutually conditioned; they influence each other. And if we accept this possibility of each epoch standing under the particular sign of a Gospel image, then perhaps it will become clear that each epoch has some special virtues of its own, as well as special vices peculiar to itself.

Perhaps we can speak conditionally of the history of virtue and the history of vice. And it would be as characteristic as speaking of the history of art, the history of government, the history of human thought, and so on. But if we look attentively at how the human spirit develops in the world, we will see that what is most characteristic for it is the alternation of enormous, almost always painful and tragic upsurges with epochs of a sort of flickering, a safeguarding of the fire, a conserving of impulses that are already dying out.

The Old Testament is in a certain sense an accurate record of how this went on in Israel. Starting from the blessed times of paradisal existence, when Adam gave names to all that existed and communed with God, there begins a long series of mankind's falls and rises. Paradisal blessedness was interrupted by the Fall. Man was forced to gain his bread in the sweat of his face. Perhaps in the sweat of his face, that is, with unbelievable spiritual efforts, he maintained a glimmer of paradisal light in his soul; he was called only to preserve, to remember and be faithful, and not to new divine reverberations, not to new paradisal visions. And even in this small task he kept falling and betraying. He sank to the very bottom of sin; in the person of Cain he raised his hand against his brother; in the person of his countless representatives he sinned and gave himself over to vice.

What could be a special virtue in this twilight of primeval mankind? Only this faithfulness to the remembrance of paradise, only a faith in the future promise, only a sober and measured walking through the vale of tears and sin.

Thus the prototype of legalism was born, the prototype of all who safeguard yesterday, who protect traditions, who make faithfulness and memory the high point of their ascent.

The human soul was perhaps frightened of boldness even then. (Was it not boldness that led our first parents out of Eden?)

The human soul even then began to limit its freedom. (Was it not freedom that caused Eve to succumb to the temptation of the serpent?)

The human soul renounced choice. Choice is only for those who fall, only for those who reject, while virtue calls for a fixed abiding in yesterday, for safeguarding, remembrance, expectation.

So began the bleak, humdrum, monotonous path of fallen mankind. And this went on for centuries. Occasionally this twilight was slashed by lightning. God would break his age-old silence, the voice of God's trumpet would burst into the freely chosen slavery and petrification, the prophets would call the world out of its ossification to a new flame, they would speak of the wrath of God and the fire that would consume the world, essentially calling again and again to choice and freedom.

The prophets were stoned. Why? Was not the glimmer of the lost paradise and the dawn of the future promise upon them? Was it not this that mankind groaned and suffered for? Was it not in the name of this that the laws were observed, the sacrifices offered, the letter safeguarded?

Why were the prophets stoned? Because mankind had learned to be afraid of freedom. Because mankind knew where this freedom had led it. It knew that with freedom of choice it might follow the prophets or it might sink into the final abyss.

No, better not to risk, not to try, not to be tempted, not to be seduced. What is due is measured precisely. A tithe of mint goes to the temple. You don't accomplish much on this path, but on the other hand you don't risk anything.

Immobility is a guarantee against new shocks, catastrophes, tragic shifts. It is also a guarantee against liberation, against melting down — all right, but it's still better, solider, calmer this way.

And so the prophets were stoned. The world slowly sank into twilight. The Ecclesiast was already composing his cries of anguish and hopelessness, the wind was returning again according to its circuits (Eccl 1:6). Dejection lay in wait for human hearts. No one believed that morning was near, and the prophets were silent.

Amidst the people of God, who repeated the words of the Ecclesiast, the guardians of their truth, of their election, the keepers of the law, of every letter of the law, the scribes, the doctors of the law, the pharisees towered up like sturdy oaks, like invincible fortresses. Man betrays, but the law will not betray. Man's soul is perverse, but the letter is fixed. And therefore the letter is higher than the soul, the sabbath is higher than man.

And in the sacred books they speak of the Messiah, the Holy One of Israel. His coming is no falsehood, and therefore let hopelessness be silent. They will keep, they will preserve the law until His glorious day. So long as nothing melts or burns, so long as everything is immobile in its dead ossification. These are the rules for the whole nation; these are also the commandments for each separate human soul. Fulfill what is written, offer the prescribed sacrifice, give to the temple what you ought to give. Keep the fasts. Do not defile yourself by communing with the unclean — and you will get your reward, or if not you then your son will get it, but you already have it, too, because you have fulfilled, because you are righteous, because you have observed the law, every letter of it, because you are not like this publican.

No doubt everyone feels this stiff-necked pharisaic truth, and can make no objection to it before the time comes. And no doubt even the contemporary human soul, every human soul, passes through this pharisaic truth, through the parched and fruitless desert of waiting, perhaps saving a last sip of water: I won't drink it, because there will be no new water.

Yes, in the desert of the spirit, in a time of terrible spiritual drought, the pharisee is justified; he alone is reasonable and thrifty, watchful and sober.

And it is not for the spendthrift, not for the one who, in the time of the great exodus, stuffs himself with manna and game, and drinks too much pure water, and dances before golden calves — it is not for him to denounce the stern thriftiness of the doctor of the law, who fasts even amidst universal famine and fulfills everything as he should. He will preserve the tables of the Covenant in the tabernacle; he will lead the souls of the people into the promised land.

How many times does the stern guardian of traditions and laws in each of our souls curse the unfaithful crowd of seducers, the violators of the law! The struggle goes on in each of us for the purity of the prescribed, for the Typikon,[28] for the letter of the law, for that which is connected with what is to come — only what is to come — the not yet incarnate promise.

When prophecy is silent in us, when our spirit is not molten, who will keep it from being dispersed and wasted if not the guardian of the law, who always stands on watch. He, too, is justified in our soul.

But he has an Accuser before whom he has no way to justify himself. There is something that displaces these laws of the

natural world, that annihilates all the righteousness of the pharisees and all the faithfulness of the doctors of the law and all the
wisdom of the scribes. And this something is fire.

Fire came down into the world. The word of God became
flesh. God became man. Not for nothing and not by chance was
this wonder, this fulfillment of the promised and the looked-for,
opposed precisely by those who were guardians of the promised,
looked-for covenant. A struggle began between the doctors of the
law and that which was higher than the law of the sabbath, with
the Son of Man. He who ate and drank with publicans and sinners, He who healed on the sabbath, He who spoke of rebuilding
the destroyed temple in three days — was He not bound to appear to them as the most terrible violator of the prescribed, of
the traditional, of the habitually saving? And they rose against
Him in the name of their age-old truth. If they did not see Him
as the Messiah, they could not feel themselves sons of the bridal
chamber, and therefore could not live according to the spirit and
power of the bridal chamber.

Fire came down into the world. Human hearts melted. The
cross of Golgotha stood on the path of the Resurrection. It would
seem that those who crucified Him, those who betrayed Him,
remained on the other side, in the old, decrepit, yielding, and
receding covenant. And on this side, with Him, remained those
of the new covenant, the fiery ones, who took the cross on their
shoulders, sanctified and transfigured by the mystery of the Resurrection — forever, until the end of the world, the members of
His Church, which Hell cannot prevail against, participants in
eternal life here in their earthly days.

But in fact Christianity preserved all the forces that were active
in the Old Testament. The same stiff-necked, indifferent, incon-
stant crowd, the same guardians of the law (now His new law),
Christian scribes, pharisees, doctors of the law — and also the
same prophets to be stoned, the same holy fools, bearers of grace
who do not fit into the framework of the law, lawless for those
who are under the law.

Properly speaking, the entire history of Christianity is the history of the extinguishing and new igniting of the fire. History

develops that way in each separate soul, and it has developed that way in the world. We know the coldness and deadness of whole epochs of Christianity, we know the flaring up and spreading of the flames of authentic Christian evangelization, we know how scribes and pharisees alternate with the initiators of new paths, and their time with broad waves of suffering, asceticism, witness, repentance, and purification.

And once again we must say in all fairness that the role of the pharisees in Christianity is not exhausted only with the extinguishing of the fire, the freezing and killing of all that is alive and ardent. They do actually and authentically watch over, keep, preserve, and bear the coffer of Christian treasures through the narrow passes of dead and self-satisfied epochs. In this sense it is not for the philistine, not for the representative of such dead epochs to attack them: they faithfully defend Christianity against the paganism that abides eternally in the world, against the cult of petty passions, prejudices, the cult of various idols, calves made of various metals — the iron calf of state power, the golden calf of economic prosperity, and so on.

But along with that they try to protect the Church against authentic Christian fervor, against all fire in general; they only preserve what is sacred to them and keep others from being nourished by it. The evaluation of pharisaism's significance and usefulness for the Church depends largely on the epoch in which the pharisees live. That evaluation therefore varies greatly and is subject to very marked fluctuations.

We stand now at the beginning of a new epoch in the Church. Much in its character is already clear. From this clarity we may judge what the Church needs at the given moment, what will contribute to her growth and ardor, and what, on the contrary, is harmful for her.

Apart from the immediate sense of the epoch, we can and must determine, in our judgments, its distinctness from the preceding epoch. This gives us the possibility of seeing what new things the Church now demands of us and what we must now free ourselves from so as not to harm her with what is old and even antiquated.

The previous epoch of the Church occupied the two hundred and some years of the Petrine period.[29] If we examine all the changes produced by Peter's reform in the life of the Church, it would be most correct to characterize them as a policy of the gradual protestantization of the Church. In a certain sense, Orthodoxy in Peter's time lived through the same experience as Catholicism in the time of Luther, the only difference being that this process never reached such intensity in Russia as in the West, never tore apart the body of the Church; it was weakened, localized, brought under obedience to Orthodox dogmas. On the other hand, it never had the character of a true religious quest, as Western Protestantism did. The Church reformers of Peter's time were least of all religious reformers. They never felt themselves to be prophets or saints. They laicized and secularized the Church; they took the world from under her jurisdiction and drove her fire into the wilderness, the forest, the sketes, into remote, isolated monasteries.

We should not close our eyes to the fact that they achieved a great deal. Synodal Orthodoxy in its external, formal manifestations actually became one of the departments of the great State of Russia. The hierarchy, decorated with state medals and ribbons, often had the psychology of an important imperial bureaucracy.

There is no need to enumerate the countless facts that speak of this secularization in the eighteenth and nineteenth centuries. We may say only that it is precisely what led to the falling away from the Church of the entire searching, educated part of the nation — the Russian intelligentsia.

If the whole Church had become what she was on the surface, what she showed herself to be in national and popular life in general, then her importance would gradually have dwindled away, and any talk of a new rebirth would be out of the question.

Yet the Church of that period also had her righteous men.

10

Insight in Wartime

As the Second World War spreads across Europe, Mother Maria, already a survivor of the Russian Civil War, reflects on the meaning of this catastrophe, now invading the lives of her neighbors and family. She probes further into the roots of this war and the feeble responses to it from the Western and Eastern churches. Though recognizing the impossibility of stopping the inferno, she holds out for the necessity of at least recognizing this terrible event in its true eschatological depth. The war is one of those events that challenge us to move beyond material complacency and to open our eyes to eternity. The fact that she would herself be consumed in this inferno makes her reflections all the more remarkable and poignant.

We people, without exception, are all heavy. Like sand mixed with water in a glass. As long as the water keeps moving, the sand is held up by it. When the water grows still, the sand sinks to the bottom. There is much in our life that stirs up this heaviness and sluggishness. We are anxious over our struggle for material existence: even such an undignified phrase as "setting oneself up" calls for some strain from us and produces a tempest in the teapot. When we are young, youth itself pulls at us, stirs us, and troubles us. Personal failures and breakdowns, various disappointments, the ruin of our hopes — all this keeps us from settling and calming down. There are more serious things still: genuine grief, irretrievable loss, above all the death of loved ones. All this annihilates our heaviness, and even our ponderousness; it suddenly leads us, imperiously and commandingly, out of this world with its laws, into another world whose laws are unknown to us.

To be convinced of the difference of these laws, it is enough to attend the funeral of some distant acquaintance. He is surrounded by people, all of them mortal and knowing what death is. But despite its being inevitable for all, these people are divided into two worlds. Some are discreetly sympathetic, polite, and matter-of-fact: how unfortunate, who would have thought, I saw him so recently, how did it happen, who was his doctor, and so on. The others — here it is not even a question of misfortune, but that the gates have suddenly opened onto eternity, all natural life has trembled and collapsed, yesterday's laws have been abolished, desires have faded, meaning has become meaningless, and another incomprehensible Meaning has grown wings on their backs. The sun has indeed been darkened, and all the dead have risen from their graves, and the veil of the temple has been rent in two. This is how the mystery of death has touched the hearts of the loving and intimate ones. Everything flies into the black maw of the fresh grave: hopes, plans, calculations, and, above all, meaning, the meaning of a whole life. If this is so, then everything has to be reconsidered, everything rejected, seen in its corruptibility and falseness.

This is what is meant by the saying, "The Lord has visited us." [30] How? By grief? By more than grief: He has suddenly revealed the true essence of things, and we have seen, on the one hand, the dead skeleton of the living, the dead carcass clothed with flesh, the dead earth and the dead sky, the deadness of the whole of creation, and on the other hand, simultaneously, we have seen the life-giving, fiery, all-filling, all-burning and comforting Spirit.

Then time — the "healer," they say, but wouldn't "deadener" be more correct? — slowly smoothes everything over. The soul becomes blind again. Again the gates of eternity are closed. Our cares, our work, our humdrum life stand before us — the sand has settled to the bottom. And again we live by the joy of small successes, by the pain of small failures, again we begin to believe that nothing is stronger than our world with its three dimensions, that what is achieved is achieved, what is saved up will prove useful in old age, everything is clear as day, though a bit boring, unless we go to birthday parties, or to the movies, or gossip about our neighbors.

Human nature, fallen, permeated with sin and its consequences, is a heavy thing.

If we try to understand what happens to the human soul in moments of terrible catastrophe, loss, or sometimes perhaps in moments of the creative transfiguration of the world, we will be able to give only one explanation of these phenomena. The gates of eternity are opened to us by way of a personal apocalypse; personal eschatology abolishes time, in which we are used to living, and space, by which we are used to measuring everything. And by somehow accepting these other laws, man is able to keep himself in eternity. The fall back into everyday life and a peaceful occupation with everyday things is by no means inevitable. Let them take their own course: eternity can be seen through them, if man is not afraid, if he does not run away from himself, does not renounce his awesome, not only human but divine-human, destiny. That is, his personal Golgotha, his personal bearing of the cross, accepted by his own free will.

This necessity of choice always stands before each man: the warmth and coziness of his earthly home, well-protected from wind and storms, or the endless space of eternity, in which there is only one firm and unquestionable thing, and this firm and unquestionable thing is the cross.

And I think that anyone who has at least once felt himself in this eternity, has at least once realized what path he is following, has seen at least once the One who walks ahead of him, will find it hard to turn from this path; to him all coziness will seem flimsy, all riches without value, all companions unnecessary, if he does not see among them the one Companion bearing the cross.

To put it more simply: a man's whole life will seem dull, worthless, meaningless to him, if it is not pierced through with the flame of eternity.

•

Such are the possibilities in each man's life. And they are also revealed to us in the life of whole nations, even of the whole of mankind, in the course of history.

Human history is also placed before the choice: either the triumph of the economic and political order, of humdrum philistine well-being, of three-dimensional space and time stretched out like a string; or the acceptance of eternity, of wings, the realization here of what is conceived *there*.

Human history is heavy, the flesh of mankind is heavy. And at the same time it is not wholly defined by this heaviness. Here and now, in our personal lives, we know that the sun can darken. Two thousand years ago the sun of all mankind darkened, and the dead left their graves, and darkness came, and the veil of the temple was rent from top to bottom before the eyes of all the people. What pierces every separate soul in the course of its earthly path, once pierced all mankind as a whole. On the cross time and eternity intersected, our history became united for a moment with what is beyond it. The Son of God lifted up His human flesh on the cross.

And later human history could follow one of two paths: either — pierced once and for all by the cross, having seen eternity once and for all, having been blinded once and for all to the temporary — it could become authentic Christian history, that is, eschatological in its essence, an exodus, a breakthrough, the eternal yearning of the winged, God-manly spirit; or it could fall down again, forget how the gates to eternity are open, even forget about eternity itself, begin to measure and to weigh, to rejoice over small national successes and be distressed at small national failures. To set up only material goals for itself and in the end proclaim that matter rules over spirit, whatever form the affirmation may take — either that existence determines consciousness, as in Marxism, or that blood gives rights or deprives of rights, as with Hitler, or that the free human soul should be enslaved to the state.

There is no doubt that post-Golgotha history fell again. Moreover, it has gone on falling in every age of its existence, in every nation, in every historical theory. The sand has settled to the bottom. The majority were not only reconciled with that, but were even convinced that it had to be so, that it could not be otherwise. The sun of the Resurrection was pushed back into the ages. Mankind felt itself not in its noonday light, but in some evening afterglow. The sky was growing darker and darker. Then there was not a gleam, not a reflection.

And then came those who maintained that this sun of the Resurrection had never even existed.

Now the forces of active materialism, of fundamental heaviness, are at work in the world.

But there were also insights during these two thousand years, variously expressed and having various causes. The chiliastic idea of the coming of the thousand-year reign of the righteous, the expectation of the end of the world among the early Christians, the expectation of the end of the world in the year 1000, and also among the Old Believers[31] in Russia under Peter the Great — despite the differences in epochs, the differences of character of the people among whom these hopes arose, they had a great deal in common, above all the conviction that this fleshly world given to us does not constitute the whole of reality, that beyond it something else begins, governed by different laws, that the kingdom of Caesar will have to give way to the Kingdom of God, that time will vanish into eternity, that the heavy gates will be opened wide to receive all mankind, and that for the sake of this longed-for hour the whole of history has existed, for it our human creativity has existed, by it our suffering will be justified, our struggle hallowed. The hour will come and lightning will flash from one end of the earth to the other, and the Son of Man will come in all His glory to judge the living and the dead.

Here a small digression is necessary in order to avoid misunderstanding. I know that the hungry man needs bread, and the weary one rest. I know that there is nothing more hypocritical than to renounce the fight for an acceptable material existence for the unfortunate, under the pretext that their material misfortunes mean nothing in the face of eternity. I think that a person can renounce any of his own rights, but he absolutely dare not renounce the rights of his neighbor. Besides that, I remember that in the most eschatological text of the Gospel, which is even known as the "Little Apocalypse" [Mt 25:31–46], Christ recalls precisely those virtues and vices that are connected with the material ministry to our neighbor. In this sense, a Christian's social task cannot be subject to any doubt.

Doubt, or not even doubt but the most terrible temptation, is caused only by the total denial of spiritual values and the affirmation of material values as the sole existing ones. We see now to what terrible dead ends this has driven the whole of mankind. I will not stop for a detailed characterization. I will say only that the universal Smerdyakov has now declared for all to hear: "If there is no God, then everything is permitted."[32] And on the basis of this affirmation he has begun to issue laws, govern states, conduct wars, enslave small nations, fill the whole space of the air with his loud and lying propaganda.

Smerdyakovism enthroned — that is the name for what is going on. And in a certain sense its actions are more logical than the actions of those nihilists of whom Soloviev[33] says: "There is no immortality, therefore let us lay down our soul for our friends." No, if there is no immortality, if the world around us does indeed constitute all there is, then it may even be impossible to draw any other conclusion than the one that is being drawn. It means the law of hatred, the struggle of all against all. It means, finally, a total denial of the cross of Golgotha, a denial of the Resurrection, an enmity for the Son of Man, who in that case made mankind live by deceit and illusion for two whole millennia. Indeed, so much precious time has been lost — one could have spent a whole extra two thousand years lawfully hating, lawfully robbing, lawfully destroying other nations and hostile classes, but instead of that one has had to act very cautiously all the time, listen to some sort of illusory and vague words, hate contrary to the law, rob, destroy, and violate contrary to the law. How natural and inevitable is the hatred of the contemporary rulers of this world for Christianity. A Christian can draw a certain bitter satisfaction from this hatred.

It seems to me that we must speak not only of what is happening on the other side of the front or in Russia. It seems to me that it is always right and useful first of all to judge our own mistakes and shortcomings or the mistakes and shortcomings of those we sympathize with. Woe to those whose shortcomings are first exposed by their enemies — their enemies will use their conclusions for their own purposes and not so that they may be essentially corrected. And so it seems to me that we should look attentively and mercilessly for the shortcomings of those we sympathize with.

There is much that alarms me on this side of the front. I look everywhere and nowhere do I find anything that would point to the possibility of any breakthrough from material life to eternity. Occasionally we come across a very uncertain expression of extremely general and diffused idealistic hopes, somewhat in the style of Dostoevsky's "sympathy with everything beautiful and lofty"[34] — but it is all rather vague. They say: "We're defending the right cause, we're fighting for the liberation of national minorities, or for the federal organization of Europe, or for democracy." These are all very valuable things, but they are not enough. Test yourselves. Imagine that you must immediately give your life for one of these goals of struggle. Try to imagine a real death. And you will understand that your own life, however modestly you evaluate its significance, is in some ultimate metaphysical sense greater than any national minorities, or paid vacations, or universal suffrage. Your life is greater and your death is greater. Test yourselves in this way, and you will see at once that apart from (and, of course, not contrary to) this real and earthly struggle, you give your life to eternity for what is connected with eternity, that you need all these freedoms and liberations because you want a free and creative spirit to reign in this heavy and enslaved world. Paid vacations, federations, and so on — these are all means, while the goal lies at a completely different depth.

So here I have this tormenting desire that there should be no half-way solutions on this side of the front, that someone should speak the ultimate truths, that these truths should set hearts on fire, that precisely these truths, loudly and clearly designated, should become the authentic, profound, religious goal of contemporary events.

And as long as that is not so, everything seems to be rather uncertain and shaky. One cannot realize creative tasks in life only by rebounding off the creative tasks of one's opponents. The ideological initiative should be in the hands of the one who wants to win, and it should be possible to clothe that initiative in various forms, from simple and easily comprehensible slogans to the ultimate truths of religious insight.

It frightens me that I do not sense it anywhere yet. Perhaps it is not surprising that people occupied with the most secularized of all human affairs — politics — do not speak to us of the ultimate values for which we must fight. That is not, so to speak, a part of their professional duties. It is natural that the marketwoman bargains at the market, the lawyer defends in court, the military commander leads an attack, the politician considers the relations between economic, diplomatic, and other forces — while the Christian preaches the Christian meaning of events that have many other meanings. And it would be bad if everybody took up some business that is not his.

But I think that such a point of view is incorrect, because in fact any business, great or small, can be done in a Christian or an anti-Christian way.

But here there is something else that troubles me. What troubles me is the Christian, and he troubles me more than any other participant in this world historical tragedy.

Before the war we heard many times about the powerful and rapid development of ecumenical movements: across the barriers of confessional differences, united by their faith in Christ, people recognized each other as brothers and wanted to act on the basis of mutual brotherly love. I'm afraid that this religious League of Nations did not pass the test any more than the political League of Nations did. I do not want to criticize what is going on too strongly and insistently. It is simply clear that it is impossible not to feel the total inadequacy of the voice of this world conscience faced with the unconscionable striving to enslave the world. And therefore, whatever attitude we take toward the ecumenical movement, it is immediately obvious that it is not to be the bearer of the Christian ideal in the modern conflict: it does not have the right voice, the right pathos, the kind of wings needed for that.

An encyclical from the pope of Rome has been published,[35] concerning the present situation in the world. It consists of carefully selected, humanly wise and noble statements. Almost nothing can be said against it. The diplomatic subtlety and refinement of its author have succeeded in making it acceptable to everyone — even to people who are far from a religious worldview. And if there are objections against it, they come not from wisdom or humaneness, not from what constituted the soul and mind of pre-war Europe, not from history, but from that sense of the end and of catastrophe in which we live. If we accept it, then it will turn out that divine law somehow coincides too much with the laws of average European humanistic liberalism, that we do not stand over an abyss, that hell and the forces that inhabit it can be fought with well-tried diplomatic treatises. It is hard to define what is unacceptable in it. Perhaps, most precisely, it is the lack of fire, the lack of a breakthrough into other worlds. To use the image I referred to earlier, this encyclical is like a kind and sympathetic acquaintance at a funeral, and by no means like a close relative, or a father for whom his son's death opens the gates to eternity, for whom everything changes, all the old burns away, and the new, winged and spirit-bearing, rends his heart with some ultimate blissful torment. I can say nothing against the pope's encyclical except that there was no great need for it.

Then comes what is most painful, most sensitive, most beloved and dear: the Orthodox man of today. Eastern hierarchs are displaying a rather great activity. The newspapers print reports of this activity only on page three. And perhaps they are right to do so: we learn from the newspapers that they sympathize with the Allies and condemn the God-hating German power. They are even much more definite than the now silent ecumenists or the much too carefully measured papal encyclical. But in all this definiteness one feels only that, for all sorts of different reasons, they have decided very firmly whom to follow, and not at all that they have decided to call people to follow them — as if they had nowhere to call anyone. In today's terrible hour they do not light up for us the steps leading to eternity. But that is the East, I will be told, which has long since abandoned the mainstream of historical life. Let us turn to ourselves.

It is hard for us Russians. Perhaps never before has history created such tangled and contradictory situations as we now find ourselves in. We may say that, whatever turn things took, under whatever circumstances, we always got hit on the head in passing. Notice how political disagreements have died out. That is because all opinions have been refuted by life. Some have been forced to admire the actions of their worst enemies: the pacifists to glorify war, the convinced fighters not to know what to fight for, the advocates of intervention to renounce intervention, the advocates of defense to dream of it. But that is all politics. Our major difficulty is in the sphere of religion. We sense the religious catastrophe that threatens the world, yet we have so long perceived religion as some noble national tradition that we now lack the energy to fill everything with its fire.

And yet we want so much to believe that precisely out of the depths of Orthodox Christianity, with its great martyrs, whom persecution removed from under the laws of this world, through the eyes of thousands and thousands of its children staring into the face of death, with the shoulders of thousands and thousands of its servants bearing the cross of Golgotha.... Crucified Orthodox Christianity is awaiting its Pascha, awaiting its resurrection in power and Spirit.

•

And now the last thing — war.

Do we accept it? Do we not accept it? Is war heroic? Is war organized crime? Is a warrior a martyr, a "passion-bearer"? Was the warrior in ancient times denied communion? Are there wars that are just, that are almost righteous? So many questions, questions which show all the contradictoriness in the very nature of war. On the one hand, war is sin and misfortune and catastrophe; on the other hand, there is something egoistically vegetarian in consistent pacifism, which makes one sick at heart.

I think that, in our notions of war, the definitions of attacking and defending sides are not sufficiently detailed. These notions are put in place at the beginning of a conflict with the aim of using them at the end for diplomatic, political, and economic purposes. But in fact the real moral or even religious distinction has not been made. If a robber breaks into a house and the one who lives in it defends himself, then later on, when the trial takes place, regardless of whether or not the robber carried out his crime, or even if the attacked one overcame him, it is still the robber who will be in the dock. And it is not that, while the robber was actually the first to attack, everything then became confused in the general fight, and it no longer even matters who began it, but what matters is who won. The right thing would be to have two different verbs to distinguish attack from defense. To say, not "France makes war" and "Germany makes war," but "Germany makes war by attacking" and "France makes war by defending," and to put the emphasis on these participles, just as we cannot say, in the case of the robber, that he and a peaceful resident began to fight, but we can say that the robber went to rob and the peaceful resident defended himself against the robbery.

I think that Christian consciousness can never be guided by the motivation of the robber; that is, to take an aggressive part in war is never acceptable for it. Much more complicated is the question of enduring war, of passive participation, of war in defense. And here I am approaching the main thing that defines the Christian attitude toward war. The strength is not in war, but in what is beyond it.

There is something in war that makes people listen — not all, but many — and suddenly, amidst the roar of cannons, the rattle of machine guns, the groaning of the wounded, they hear something else, they hear the distant, warning trumpet of the archangel.

We know the results of great wars: essentially they even out the losses of the victors and the vanquished, they let blood from both sides. Statistics count up the numbers of dead and wounded in tens and hundreds of thousands, if not in millions; statistics tell us of incredible material impoverishment, of billions blown up in the air, sent to the bottom of the sea, burned, destroyed, annihilated.

There is also, in a sense, a more terrible phenomenon, which cannot be accounted for by statistics: it is the brutalization of nations, the lowering of the cultural level, the loss of creative ability — the decadence of souls. Every war throws the whole of mankind back. An important role in this process is played by the destruction of the youngest and most creatively active strata of society, as well as by the psychological deformation of those who remain alive and physically whole. In a certain sense, we can maintain the paradox that every war, however it may end, by the very fact of its specific influence creates the possibility, even the inevitability, of the next war. It educates the future cadres, who will want at all costs to make war. Enough has been said for us to know what our attitude toward war ought to be. There can be no two opinions here. What's more, what has been said can be multiplied by thousands and thousands of new arguments against war.

And yet, while maintaining the truth of all these arguments, I still say with full conviction that there is something in war that constitutes our only chance, as it were, in mankind's current situation. That does not mean that we should want it. But, once it has broken out, it should be made use of. I think that now, as war spontaneously overtakes nation after nation and it is hard to foresee who else will be drawn into it, and generally hard to foresee anything in the political, diplomatic, economic, and even purely military sphere, there is one sphere in which there is nothing to foresee — it is all so clear. This is the sphere of the human spirit.

The war demands of us, more than ever, that we mobilize absolutely all our spiritual powers and abilities. And we must understand what mobilization means. If a soldier, on being mobilized, must leave his beloved family, his habitual occupation, even his vocation, must step out of the time in which he lived, as it were, and switch over into some other time, if everything is taken from the mobilized soldier and everything is demanded of him, then our Christian mobilization should present a man with no lesser demands. In our time Christ and the life-giving Holy Spirit demand the whole person. The only difference from state mobilization is that the state enforces mobilization, while our faith waits for volunteers. And, in my view, the destiny of mankind depends on whether these volunteers exist and, if they do, how great their energy is, how ready they are for sacrifice.

In fact, war is the wing of death spread over the world, war is for thousands and thousands of people an open gate to eternity, war is the collapse of philistine order, coziness, and stability. War is a call, war is an insight.

And there are two ways to respond to this call, to this sounding of the archangel's trumpet. We can respond as a respectable visitor at a funeral service responds to death, as something sad but extraneous. That is the usual response. If it sometimes does not amaze us, that is only because we are somehow used to everything.

In fact, if you think of it, should we not be amazed by any issue of an illustrated magazine in which there is a picture of sailors drowning in the sea — human lives perishing — or of a dead soldier in the snow, frozen, his open, glassy eyes staring at the sky, and on the next page some movie actress, pampered, well-scrubbed, all made-up, smiling as she performs some physical exercise? Or a caricature of Parisian *midinettes,* or something else from that other, already submerged world? These juxtapositions are innocent, because their absurdity does not amaze editors or readers, but at the same time cynical, I would even say sinister.

Enough, enough. Right now, at this moment, I know that hundreds of people are face to face with what is most serious, with Seriousness itself — with death; I know that thousands and thousands of people are waiting their turn. I know that mothers are watching for the mailman and tremble when a letter comes a day late; I know that wives and children feel the breath of war in their peaceful homes.

And, finally, I know, I know with all my being, with all my faith, with all the spiritual force granted to the human soul, that at this moment God is visiting His world. And the world can receive that visit, open its heart — "ready, ready is my heart" — and then in an instant our temporary and fallen life will unite with the depths of eternity, then our human cross will become the likeness of the God-man's cross, then within our deathly affliction itself we will see the white garments of the angel who will announce to us: "He who was dead is no longer in the tomb." Then mankind will enter into the paschal joy of the Resurrection.

Or else...Maybe it will not even be worse than before, but merely the same as before. Once again — and how often has it been? — we will have fallen, we will not have accepted, we will not have found the path to transfiguration.

The old, sad, dusty earth races through the empty sky into eternal emptiness. Death-bound mankind rejoices over small successes and weeps over small failures, renouncing its election, painstakingly and assiduously pulling the coffin lid over its head.

11

Types of Religious Life

Though written in 1937, this essay, arguably one of Mother Maria's most significant writings, was discovered only in 1996 by Hélène Klepinin-Arjakovsky in the archive of Sophia Pilenko (Mother Maria's mother). While based on very specific groups and tendencies within the Russian Orthodox Church, nonetheless Mother Maria's analysis of five types of Christian faith and practice remain widely relevant today, even beyond the original Russian Orthodox context. In turn she posits and offers a critique of four religious types: synodal, ritualist, aesthetical, and ascetical, before presenting her own ideal, which she calls the evangelical type.

Of all the types, the one most tied to Russian history is the "synodal" model, which refers to the long period in Russian history when the Orthodox Church was administered as a department of the tsarist state. But even here, one can recognize the tendency among many Christians to cling to a "traditional" and seemingly "unchangeable" vision of an institution's identity and piety. Such a model might be recognized under the more familiar word "Christendom." The discerning reader, regardless of background, will surely also recognize the Roman Catholic, Episcopalian, Baptist, or other versions of the other "types" depicted here: the ritualist, aesthetical, ascetical. In each case she offers a fairly biting critique of approaches to religious practice that substitute the love of tradition, order, doctrine, liturgy, or form for the underlying Spirit of God.

Mother Maria's last type, the "evangelical," is not to be identified with the modern Protestant variety, whether that is identified as Bible-based, culturally and ethically conservative, or openly and emotionally expressive. Rather, what she means by the "Gospel" type is a more authentic Christianity of the sort already reflected in the preceding writings. In this type, liturgy and hierarchy, dogma and tradition all have their place, but here we seek first God and God's kingdom, and recognize Him foremost in the face of the brother or sister before us. Love of God is love of the neighbor. The liturgy we celebrate in church is the liturgy we must live on the street, in our homes, in loving service to the neighbor. Again, the relevance of this model is not confined to the Orthodox Church. Indeed, Mother Maria's vision points to a truly ecumenical convergence available to Christians of all backgrounds and traditions, and it is this challenge, among others, that gives her voice such an enduring and urgent relevance.

If we study carefully the historical situation in which we find ourselves or, more accurately, those types of piety which our present-day situation has produced, we can discern, objectively and dispassionately, various categories of people who do not understand man's religious calling in the same way. Each category has its own positive and negative characteristics, and it is entirely possible that only the sum of them would give a proper overview of the multifaceted nature of Christian life. On the other hand, when classifying types of religious life within Orthodoxy one must always bear in mind that alongside the completely distinctive representatives of one or another type, the majority of people will represent some kind of combination of two or even more types of religious life. It is very difficult to remain within the framework of impartiality and objectivity when classifying and defining these types, because in reality individuals are attracted to their own concept of Christianity and repel any understanding that is not their own. In this article I can only say that I wish to make every effort to avoid such partiality.

The Five Types

If, while observing Orthodox believers, you enter into conversation with them and read the various Orthodox books and journals devoted to spiritual questions, you are at once struck by the incredible multifacetedness of their understanding of the spiritual life. If, however, you make an attempt to classify this variety into more or less closely defined categories, then I would say that at this given moment within Orthodoxy there are five types of piety: (1) synodal, (2) ritualist, (3) aesthetic, (4) ascetic, and (5) evangelical. To be sure, such a classification is to some extent arbitrary. Life is much more complex than this, and it is very likely that there are other categories that I was unable to discern. But even this arbitrary classification is of great help in understanding many events in our lives. To a certain degree, it also permits us to understand our own personal sympathies and antipathies, our own spiritual path. Each spiritual type has its own, at times very complicated, history, its own coming into being; each is determined by the diverse circumstances of its origin. We find ourselves in one or another group not only as the result of some internal inclination, but also because we are, to some extent, predetermined for it by the milieu from which we come, by our upbringing, education, and other influences. I will attempt to characterize each category from the point of its historical origins, its moral attributes, its way of life (and even its special skills), the extent of its spread, the creative potential contained within it, and its relationship to the current problems of Church life.

The Synodal Type

The Russian emigration flowed into Europe, one might say, before it had cooled down after its struggle, still seething with passionate fury at having been deprived of the ideals of that great Russian land, of the "White" idea, etc. It carried with it not only its own miserable baggage, not only its bayonets and regimental banners, but portable churches with iconostases made out of cloth stretched over wooden frames, sacred vessels, and vestments. And having landed on foreign soil, it set up not only branches of the All-Forces Union, but its own churches. For many the Church was a vital requirement for their souls. For many, a kind of inescapable attribute of the idea of Russia as a Great Power, without which it was difficult to speak of nationalism, of loyalty to the traditions and ordinances of the past. The Church was a reliable and recognized political and patriotic symbol. Somehow its inner meaning did not attract much attention. The important thing was to commemorate the anniversaries of the tragic deaths of national heroes or the anniversaries of the establishment of glorious regiments. In church it was possible to organize solemn, sober demonstrations of one's unity, one's loyalty. One could participate in services of intercession for the departed, kneel on one knee during the singing of "Memory Eternal,"[36] gather around the senior officer present. Very often a considerable degree of ingenuity and energy was expended in fashioning a censer or seven-branched candlestand out of empty food cans, or in converting some drafty barracks into a church. The existence of the Church was essential, but the motivations for this need often were of a national rather than ecclesial character.

If we try to discover the origin of such an attitude, it isn't hard to find its roots in the previous ecclesiastical epoch, the so-called "synodal period" of the Church. From the time of Peter the Great our Russian Orthodox Church became an attribute of the autocratic Russian state, one department among other departments, and took its place in the system of government institutions, absorbing into itself the government's ideas, experiences, and the taste of power. The state granted it protection, punished offenses against the Church, and in return demanded condemnation for offenses against the state. The state appointed the Church's hierarchs, kept an eye on their activities with the help of the chief procurator, assigned administrative tasks to the Church, and made it a party to its political expectations and ideals.

After two hundred years of such a system's existence the inner structure of the Church was itself changed. Spiritual life was pushed into the background, while on the surface one had an official state-sanctioned religiosity, with certificates being issued to civil functionaries certifying that they had been to Confession and Communion, since without such a certificate the functionary could not be considered a loyal subject from the state's point of view. This system led to the creation of a special religious psychology, a special religious type, with a particular kind of moral foundation, a particular kind of churchmanship, and a special way of life. For generation after generation people were schooled in the idea that the Church is of utmost importance, something absolutely necessary, but still it was only an attribute of the state. Piety was one of the state virtues, necessary only because the state had need of pious people. The priest was an overseer appointed by the state to look after the correct performance of religious functions by loyal Russian subjects. As such he was a respected figure, but nevertheless as an individual he enjoyed no more respect than did other functionaries who looked after social order, the armed forces, finances, etc.

The synodal period saw a completely astounding attitude toward the clergy, the total absence of any distinctive status, and even a tendency to treat them as inferior, not allowing them entry into so-called "society." People went to Confession once a year because this was what was required. They got married in church, they baptized their children, buried their dead, stood through prayers of intercession on royal festivals, and — when they were particularly pious — served akathists.[37] But the church was something quite separate from the rest of life. People went there when it was called for — and it was certainly not called for to overdo one's churchiness. This was perhaps done only by the Slavophils,[38] who by their conduct slightly modified the established, formal, official tone of polite relationship toward the Church. It is only natural that the synodal type of piety was grounded, in the first instance, on the cadres of the Petersburg ministerial bureaucracy, that it was linked specifically with bureaucracy and so was spread throughout Russia through provincial bureaucratic centers to the local representatives of state authority.

This whole system was preordained so that the most religiously gifted and fervent believers would find in it no place for themselves. They either went to monasteries, seeking to separate themselves completely from all superficial Church activity, or they simply revolted, frequently protesting not only against the Church's institutional system but against the Church itself. This is the origin of the anti-religious fanaticism of our revolutionaries, which so resembled, in its earliest manifestations, the flaming passion of true religious life. It attracted to itself all those who thirsted for inner ascetic endeavor, for sacrifice, selfless service, and disinterested love — all of which the official state Church could not offer. It must be said that during the synodal period even the monasteries succumbed to this general process of disintegration of the spiritual life. The all-powerful arm of the state was extended over them, over their morals and way of life, and they were turned into official cells of the overall ecclesiastical establishment.

Thus there remained in the Church for the most part either those who were lukewarm, those who could keep their religious impulses under control, or those who could channel their spiritual needs into the system of state values. In this way a system of moral ideals developed. No doubt what was held in the greatest esteem was good order, a respect for the law, a certain reserve, along with rather firmly expressed feelings of obligation, respect for one's elders, a condescending concern for one's juniors, honesty, love of Fatherland, a reverence for authority, etc. No special exertions were required. Creativity was suppressed in the interests of good order and the general purposes of the state machine. Religious zealots somehow failed to appear in provincial cathedral churches.

Here there were people of a different sort: rectors, calm, businesslike cathedral archpriests thoroughly familiar with the Divine Services, who made every effort to conduct them solemnly and with grandeur in splendid and magnificent temples, superb administrators and organizers, custodians of Church property, official functionaries of the synodal establishment, honorable people, conscientious, but uninspiring and uncreative.

And the cathedrals — the crowning expression of the synodal architectural craftsmanship — were overwhelming in their massiveness, their spaciousness, their gilt and marble, with huge

cupolas, resonant echoes, immense royal doors, and costly vestments. Colossal choirs performed special Italianate and secularized ecclesiastical chants. The images on the icons could hardly
be seen, having been encased in gold and silver covers. The dea-
con could hardly lift the book of the Gospels, with its heavy
binding, and he read it in such a way that at times it was impossible to understand a single word. But it was not his job to
make the reading understandable: he had to begin with a kind of
unimaginably low rumble and end in a window-rattling bellow,
showing off the mighty power of his voice. Everything had but
a single purpose, everything was in harmony with each aspect of
the epoch's churchmanship, everything had as its aim a display of
the power, wealth, and indestructibility of the Orthodox Church
and the great Russian state that protected her.

How widespread was this kind of ecclesiastical psychology?
Certainly, one ought not to imagine that this was the only type
of religious consciousness, but without a doubt any other kind
would have to be searched for diligently, since the "official" type
was so overpowering. This is especially clear if we take into account that alongside such an understanding of ecclesiastical life
and religious ways, we developed our own intense form of atheism. These people, as Soloviev accurately observed, laid down
their souls for their friends while believing that man evolved from
apes. Thus it was possible to find an outlet for love, sacrifice, and
heroic deeds outside church walls.

But within the Church anything that was different, was, by
that fact alone, in opposition: it flowed against the current and
was persecuted and belittled. This ecclesiastical psychology was
based on a very solid way of life, and this way of life, in turn, was
nourished by it. Tradition permeated everything, from prayer to
the kitchen. From what has been said it should be obvious that
on such soil one could hardly expect to see creative forces grow.

Here everything is channeled toward conservation, to the preservation of the foundations, to the repetition of feelings, words,
and gestures. Creativity demands some new kind of challenge;
here there was none, neither in the field of ideas, nor in the field
of arts, nor in the way of life. Everything was strongly guarded

and protected. Innovation was not permitted. There was no need for any creative principle. The synodal type of religious life, which promoted other values along with spiritual ones, namely, those of the state, of a way of life, and of a particular tradition, not only distorted and confused the hierarchy of values, but often simply replaced Christian love with an egotistical love for the things of this world. It is difficult, even impossible to see Christ, to experience a christianization of life, where the principle of the secularization of the Church is openly proclaimed. This type of piety was not up to the difficult task of rendering to God what is God's and what is Caesar's to Caesar.

During its lengthy existence it more and more frequently let Caesar triumph. Through it the Roman emperor conquered Christ, not in the circus arena, not in the catacombs, but at the very moment when he recognized the Heavenly King: at that very moment the subversion of Christ's commandments by the commandments of the secular state began. One can acquire synodal piety through one's education, through habit and custom, but in no way can one acquire it through a desire to follow in the footsteps of Christ. From a historical point of view this orderly system had already begun to show cracks by the end of the nineteenth century. Suddenly a guest appeared in the Church, and not an entirely welcome one: the Russian intelligentsia. We shall speak more about its role later, but at first this role was only shallowly rooted in the Church's life. It was more a phenomenon on the fringes of the Church.

Everything changed decisively from the moment of the February [1917] revolution and, in the Church, these changes were reflected in the All-Russian Church Council [of 1917–18] and the restoration of the Patriarchate.[39]

However important these changes were to the Church's historical way of life, they could not, of course, suddenly change people's psychology and refashion the temper of their souls. Because of this the emigration brought with it into foreign lands memories of the Russian Church's synodal period, its way of life, its art, its clergy, its understanding of the Church's role and significance in the overall patriotic scheme. It is very likely that even now the synodal type of piety predominates. This is easy to demonstrate if we bear in mind that the whole of the Karlovatsky group[40] in our Church lives precisely in accordance with this ideology, uniting Church and state, preserving the old traditions, not wanting to take cognizance of the new conditions of life and continuing to preach Caesaropapism. Not everyone who belonged to the synodal psychology was attracted exclusively to that special group.

Everywhere, in spacious cathedrals and in provincial makeshift churches, we can find people who confess their membership in the Orthodox Church and along with this believe that the Church is simply a necessary attribute of Russian sovereignty.

It is difficult to have two views on whether this psychology has any correlation with the current problems of the Church's life. In the first place, life today demands creative efforts from us so urgently that no grouping which lacks a creative agenda can expect to succeed. Moreover, there is no doubt but that on the historical plane the synodal period has come to an end with no possibility of return; there is no basis for assuming that the psychology which it engendered can survive it for long. In this sense it is not important how we assess such a religious type. Only one thing is important: without a doubt it is dying and has no future. The future challenges the Church with such complex, new, and crucial problems that it is difficult to say off hand to which religious type it will give the possibility to prove itself and reveal itself in a creative manner.

The Ritual Type

The next type of religious life, that of the strict ritualist,[41] bears traces of an entirely different origin. Compared to the synodal type it is archaic, but it has never died out. It intertwined itself with synodal piety, standing over against it, but has never struggled with it. Synodal piety encountered strict ritualism in the Church from the moment of its own origin, since the whole of Muscovite Rus' was permeated with its spirit. The Old Believer schism grew out of it and absorbed its strengths into itself.

By modifying itself and becoming more complex, it has endured even down to our time. It is, perhaps, the most frightening and inert remnant inherited from Muscovite Rus'.

There is no doubt that the creative and theological level of Muscovite piety was extremely weak. Moscow adopted many things from Byzantium, but somehow managed to miss its creative intensity. Moscow reforged all the turbulent and antinomian vibrancy of the Byzantine genius into an immovable form, a cult of the letter, a cult of tradition, a repetitious rhythmical gesture. Moscow was able not only to freeze its Byzantine heritage, but even managed to dry up its biblical heritage, ossifying it and depriving it of its grace-filled, living spirit. In the words of an ancient prophet, it started to pile up "commandment upon commandment, rule upon rule." It perceived the splendid flow of Byzantine rhetoric as something that should not be touched, introducing it into its own obligatory order of service, ritualizing every impulse, enveloping every religious lyric with the form of law.

The extreme expression of this stagnant, splendid, immovable, protective spirit was the Old Believer schism. In a sense it has great merits: it has preserved for us examples of ancient icon painting, it has preserved the ancient chant, it has kept in a safe place, away from the flow of life, one moment in the development of piety and fixed it once and for all. But with all this it confused the hierarchy of values of the Christian way of life, preferring torture and even death not only in defense of the two-fingered sign of the cross, but for the right to write "Isus" instead of "Iisus."

Here it is not a question simply of illiteracy. The issue is much more serious, as became obvious in the following period. We are dealing here with belief in a particular kind of magic, not just of a word, a name, but of each letter that makes up the name [i.e., Isus]. A frightful retribution has been visited upon the Old Believers for their treatment of Christ's truth. Go into an Old Believer meeting house. It contains everything that they have held dear throughout their whole history. It has priceless icons in the ancient style; it has ancient books; it resounds to a special chant sung according to the old "hook" notation — all those things for which they struggled and endured martyrdom. It lacks only one thing: its magnificent iconostasis, completely covered with icons in massive metalwork covers, shelters nothing, it preserves nothing. For behind the iconostasis is a blank wall, to which the iconostasis is fixed. There is no sanctuary, no altar table, no table of oblation, since there is no Mystery, no Sacrament.

Everything has been preserved except the living spirit of the Church, its mysterious God-manly life. Only the splendid form remains.

One must give some thought to this phenomenon. Here people have received a punishment for their victory, for having attained their aims. Having once distorted Christ's truth, they were left with its empty shell. We should think about this every time we are tempted to replace spirit with form, love with ritual. In this temptation the same danger lies in wait for us: to be left with form and ritual, but to forfeit spirit and love. It is very likely that this symbol of a Church without a sanctuary is often reflected in human souls.

While losing the living spirit of Christianity, the Church of the eighteenth and nineteenth centuries has not been able to extirpate within itself that Moscow spirit of ritual correctness: what is prescribed, what is permitted, what is to be preserved. Moreover, the human soul, frequently stifled in the official, cold, state-sanctioned Synodal Church and not finding any way to some kind of living source of faith, would flee from the synodal understanding of piety into the arms of ritual correctness, placing this in opposition to official conventionality. Ritual correctness has something in common with ecclesiastical aesthetics and asceticism, but in its essence it is something different. It is simply that the stress is not placed there.

What is the moral temper of the strict ritualist? What is his spiritual make-up? His greatest desire is for absolute spiritual order, the complete subordination of the inner life to an external rhythm, which has been elaborately worked out in the minutest detail. This external rhythm encompasses everything within itself. Outside the Church he knows the spiritual significance of every detail of life. He keeps the fast. He lives day in and day out following the Church's cycle of services. He lights vigil lamps at prescribed times. He makes the sign of the cross correctly. In Church he likewise stifles any impulse, permits no deviation from the established gestures. He kneels at the proper moment during services, he bows and crosses himself at the proper time. He knows for certain that one doesn't kneel from Pascha to Pentecost, he knows how many times he will go to Confession during the year, and above all he has mastered the Order of Services to the minutest detail. He is angry and indignant if anything is omitted during Church services, because that is not to be done. Yet at the same time he is completely indifferent when what is being read is incomprehensible or when it is being read too rapidly. This is not the person who prefers memorial services, services of intercession, and akathists over others. No, his most loved services are the rarest ones, above all those of Great Lent. He especially delights in the complexity of services when a fixed feast coincides with a movable one, for example, when the Annunciation falls during the last days of Holy Week.

For him the form and structure of the service frequently overshadows the inner content of individual prayers. He is most certainly a fanatical champion of Church Slavonic. For him the use of Russian in Church is almost blasphemy. He loves Slavonic because he is used to it and does not want to change even the obviously unsatisfactory, ungrammatical, and inaccurate translations from the Greek. The lengthy readings by the *psalomshchik* [reader] immerse him in a particular atmosphere of piety, giving a specific rhythm to his spiritual life. This is what is important, what he really wants. The content does not really interest him. His prayers are lengthy, and he has an established and unchanging "rule" for them. This rule frequently requires the repetition of the same prayers, and always in the same place. The Gospel and the Lord's Prayer are not singled out within the general structure of his rule: they are merely a part of a harmonious whole established once and for all.

If you tell him that you don't understand something, either in essence or because the *psalomshchik* is reading too rapidly, he will answer that it isn't necessary to understand; it is only necessary to achieve a particular atmosphere of piety during which occasional words come through clearly which are understandable and necessary for you.

The spiritual life of such a person is worked out in the smallest detail. He knows the special technique for bringing oneself to a particular spiritual state. He is able to teach you how to breathe, in what position to maintain your body during prayer, and whether the legs should be warm or cool.

If one analyzes this special phenomenon, it becomes clear that basically it does not depend on Eastern Christianity, for one senses here a sort of Dervishism and echoes of Hinduism and, more significantly, a passionate belief in the magic of the word and of combinations of words, of gestures and sequences of gestures. There is no doubt but that this belief in magic has beneath it very real roots. Much can be achieved with this method: a very great degree of self-discipline, a large measure of control over oneself and over all the chaos of the human soul, even control over others, a complete structuring of one's inner and outer life — even a certain kind of inspiration under the law.

But one thing which this way of life does not achieve is, of course, love. One can "speak with the tongues of men and of angels, and have not love" (1 Cor 13:1). To be sure, acts of love and benevolence enter into the rhythm of the strict ritualist's life. The strict ritualist knows that he must help the poor, especially during Great Lent. In his time he has sent *kalachi* [white bread loaves] to those confined in prison. He might even organize a benefit, build almshouses, and put on dinners for his poorer brethren. But the basic motive for such activity is that it is prescribed, that it enters into the general rhythm of his life, that it has become part of his ritualist concept of things. In this sense he has a greatly developed feeling of obligation and obedience. Thus his relationship to others is determined by a self-imposed obligation and is not based on a spontaneous feeling of love toward them.

At the present time this type of piety has rather a tendency to grow and spread. This expansion can easily be explained if we take into account all the misfortune, abandonment, neglect, and exhaustion of the contemporary human soul. This soul is not looking for a challenge: it is afraid any challenge will be a burden beyond its strength; it can no longer either seek anything or accept the possibility of being disenchanted. The austere and rarefied air of sacrificial love is beyond its strength. If life has passed it by and given it no external well-being, no external stability, then it turns with special zeal toward internal well-being, toward the utter determinacy and legitimacy of its inner world. It throws over the chaos a sturdy cover of what is prescribed, what is permitted, and the chaos ceases to torment it. It knows the effectiveness of magical incantations, often expressed in incomprehensible syllables. Like the dervish, it knows the power of a gesture or a pose. It feels protected and tranquil. All these particularities of the strict ritualist path determine its growth in our times. In all likelihood a long period of development awaits it.

It must be noted here that from another point of view also our era may expect to see the further development of strict ritualism. We can see today an almost universal thirst for definite, concrete directives of some kind: how to believe, what to fight for, how to behave oneself, how to speak, how to think. We see that the world has a thirst for authoritative leaders who can lead a blind and loyal mass behind them.

We know of the existence of the most frightful dictatorship that has ever been, the tyranny of ideas. The infallible center — the Party, for example, or the Leader, the Führer — wills that we think and act in one way, and the individual, who believes in the infallibility of the directive, easily, with astounding and incomprehensible ease, restructures his inner world to correspond with this directive. We know of the presence of state-imposed philosophies and worldviews. If we grant that somewhere the Church might become, if not supportive then at least tolerant of this, it will then be inundated with new cadres of people who have been brought up on mandatory directives, and strict ritualism will immediately teach them which path they must follow, where there is less doubt, where the directives are more precise and better regulate one's whole life, where, finally, the entire chaos of the human soul is tamed and driven into the allotted cages. Here the success of ritualism is absolutely foreordained.

But at the same time it is impossible to speak of its creative possibilities. Its very principle, a constant repetition of rules, words, and gestures, excludes any possibility of creative tension. From ancient times strict ritualism has been opposed to prophecy and creativity. Its task was to preserve and to repeat, and not to tear down and rebuild. If it does, in fact, come out on top, then this will mean the extinction of the creative spirit and freedom in the Church for many decades.

The main question, however, which should be addressed to strict ritualism is this: how does it respond to Christ's commandments concerning love for God and love for other people? Does it have a place for them? Where within it is the person to whom Christ came down? If it can be granted that very often there is expressed in it its own kind of love for God, it is difficult to see in what way it expresses itself in love for people.

Christ, who turned away from scribes and pharisees, Christ, who approached prostitutes, publicans, and sinners, can hardly be the teacher of those who are afraid to soil their pristine garments, who are completely devoted to the letter, who live only by the rules, and who govern their whole life according to the rules. Such people consider themselves in good spiritual health because they observe everything that is prescribed by spiritual hygiene. But Christ told us, it is not the healthy who are in need of a physician, but the sick. In fact, we have today two citadels of such an Orthodoxy — traditional, canon-based, patristic, and paternal Orthodoxy: Athos and Valaam.[42] A world of people far removed from our bustle and our sins, a world of faithful servants of Christ, a world of knowledge of God and contemplation.

And what do you suppose most upsets this world of sanctity? How does it regard the present calamities that are tearing us apart, the new teachings, heresies perhaps, the destitution, the destruction, and the persecution of the Church, the martyrs in Russia, the trampling down of belief throughout the whole world, the lack of love? Is this what most alarms these islands of the elect, these pinnacles of the Orthodox spirit? Not at all. What strikes them as the most important, the most vital, the most burning issue of the day, is the question of the use of the Old or New

Calendar in divine services. It is this that splits them into factions, this that leads them to condemn those who think otherwise than they do, this that defines their measure of things.

It is difficult to speak about love against this background, since love somehow falls outside both the New and the Old Calendar. We can, of course, state that the Son of Man was Lord of the Sabbath, and that he violated that Sabbath precisely in the name of love. But where they do not violate it, where they cannot violate it, this is because there is no "in the name" nor is there love. Strict ritualism reveals itself here to be a slave of the Sabbath and not the way of the Son of Man. And truly there is something threatening and ominous here, precisely because in Athos and Valaam, the ancient centers of traditional Orthodox spirituality, a person can find an answer to only one question out of all those that are raised by life: whether the Church must live according to the Old Calendar or the New. Instead of the Living God, instead of Christ crucified and risen, do we not have here a new idol, a new form of paganism, which is manifested in arguments over calendars, rubrics, rules, and prohibitions — a Sabbath which triumphs over the Son of Man? Idolatry in the world is frightening when it betrays Christ in the name of the state, the nation, a social idea, or petty bourgeois comfort and well-being. Still more frightening, however, is idolatry within the Church, when it replaces Christ's love with the keeping of the Sabbath.

The Aesthetic Type

It is difficult to trace the origins of the aesthetic type of piety. It has probably had its representatives during all ages, easing off slightly only at times when the Church was faced with challenges causing great spiritual tension, when the Church was being shaken by internal struggles, when it was being persecuted, and when it was obliged to defend the very essence of Christianity. Even the origin of Christianity in Kievan Rus', according to the ancient legend, was determined by a well-known act of aesthetic piety. St. Vladimir compared religions not on the substance of their inner content, but on the strength of the impression made

by their external forms. Thus he chose Orthodoxy for the beauty
of its singing, for the grandeur of its rites, and for that aesthetic experience which so shook him. The writers of Muscovite
Rus' have produced long and moving descriptions of Orthodoxy's beauty. Even the nineteenth century, not known for any
special aesthetic sensitivity, produced such a great example of an
Orthodox aesthete as Konstantin Leontiev,[43] for whom beauty
contained within it the measure of truth and who, having rejected
the religiously empty bourgeois world because it was monstrous,
reached out to Orthodoxy because in it there was beauty.

No wonder, then, that in the twentieth century, when two fac-
tors converged — a bright and talented outburst of aestheticism
among the cultural upper stratum of Russian life and the entry
of a large number of people from that cultural stratum into the
Church — the aesthetic type of piety was almost overwhelming
and determined many things. For a start, it identified very great
treasures from the past. Aesthetics has always been linked with
a kind of cult of antiquity, with a kind of archaeology. It is not
surprising, therefore, that during the period when it flourished,
ancient Russian art was rediscovered. Ancient icons were found,
restored, and studied; museums of iconography were established;
schools of iconography were defined and described; Rublev and
others began to be appreciated. The ancient chant began to be restored. Kievan and Valaam chants found their way back into the
repertoire of church singing; church architecture became better
known thanks to a great number of publications on the history
of art. Without a doubt, all these are positive achievements.

But alongside this aesthetic approach to religion there began to
grow a particular moral mind-set, whose characteristics are quite
easy to detect. Beauty and the appreciation of beauty are always
the province of a small minority. This explains the unavoidable
cultural elitism of any aesthetic stance. When defending aesthetic
values, the aesthete divides the whole world into friends who
understand and appreciate his values, and enemies, the profane
crowd. Imagining that the foundation of church life is its beauty,
then he divides all humankind into a "little flock" with special
aesthetic sensitivity, and the mass of those unworthies to be found

beyond the pale. In the mind of such an individual, the mystery of the Church belongs only to the elect. Not only will prostitutes and sinners never sit at the feet of Christ, but all those who are too simple and unrefined will likewise be excluded, so that the aesthete himself may find satisfaction through the lofty aesthetic beauty of the divine services, and so on.

Because the aesthete takes aesthetics to be the sole criterion of what is proper, the sole measure of things, he thinks of himself as part of some kind of intricate composition and feels obliged not to spoil it, not to disturb it. He accepts its general rhythm, but then introduces that rhythm into his own inner life. Like the strict ritualist, he structures his own personal way of life and sees in this his greatest virtue. The aesthete is always attracted by the archaic. At times he may even be attracted to a type of popular, peasant artistry. From this there develops a subtle attraction toward specific portions of the services, toward individual hymns, the Great Canon of St. Andrew of Crete, and so forth. Often the artistic value of that material is assessed, and, if there isn't any, that is taken into account and he is then entranced by its antiquity, or struck by its stately composition, or by the rhythmic success of the whole of the divine service.

Aesthetic criteria gradually replace the spiritual and eventually displace all other considerations. The people in the Church are looked upon as either a crowd of worshipers, props needed for the proper rhythm of worship, or as tedious and annoying barbarians who, by their ignorance, clumsiness, and, occasionally, by their personal sorrows and special needs, encroach upon the general grandeur and orderliness of the service.

The aesthete loses himself in clouds of incense, delights in the ancient chants, admires the severity and restraint of the Novgorod style of iconography. He will condescendingly take note of the somewhat naive wording of a hymn. He has partaken in everything, he is sated, afraid to spill his treasure. He is afraid of tasteless detail, of the human woes that provoke sympathy; he is afraid of human weakness, which provokes disgust. All in all, he doesn't like the petty, confused, disorganized world of the human soul. No doubt it would be difficult to find love within the aesthetic type of religious life. Nor, it would seem, is there even a place in it for hatred. There is only that cold, exacting contempt for the profane crowd and an ecstatic admiration for beauty. There is a dryness, often verging on formalism. There is a concern for the preservation of oneself and one's own world, which is so well structured and harmonized, from the intrusion of anything that might offend or upset that harmony. Even fiery souls will gradually cool down through the inescapable chill of aestheticism (Konstantin Leontiev, for example, had a fiery soul by nature). He insists on putting a chill on everything that surrounds him, looking for some kind of eternal ice, for some eternal pole of beauty, for an eternal Northern Lights.

The strangest and most incredible thing of all is the possibility of the spread of the aesthetic type of piety among Russians, whose souls, as a rule, are lacking in harmony, measure, and form. One might think that their fiery temperament, their pithy sayings, and, at times, their chaotic style would serve to guarantee that aestheticism is no danger for them. Perhaps there is a kind of "law of contradiction" in effect here, forcing a person to seek in a worldview what will supplement his inner characteristics rather than express them. Perhaps he finds it impossible to get along with his inner chaos, to endure it, and, as a result, he moves toward the other extreme. And yet one often sees, much more frequently than one might imagine, a strange suppression of that flame, almost amounting to spiritual suicide, which changes fire into ice — an impulse toward immobility, an all-out search for a rhythm of external, given forms. There is no doubt, of course, that the aesthetic type of Orthodox piety, which by its very nature belongs to the higher cultural levels of the Russian people, cannot count on a numerically widespread dissemination.

The issue, however, is not numbers, but precisely the quality, in a cultural sense, of these repositories of Orthodox aesthetics. In spite of their small numbers they could have and still can have a strong influence on the life of the Church in all its aspects. What is the nature of this influence? How great is its creative impulse? Here one must speak about one extraordinary, paradoxical fact. The true guardians of creative activity, throughout the most diverse ages, nations, and peoples, have always valued the genius or talent of others. These aesthetes, who were subtle critics and experts in the most minute details and nuances of the various artistic schools, have never at any time or anywhere provided creative leadership themselves, perhaps just because they were so subtly and so intensely assessing the works of others. This has always resulted in a particular personal psychology shared by museum curators, collectors, experts, and catalogers, but not by creative artists.

Creativity, even that which produces the most subtle works of art, is in its essence something rather crude. Creativity, which aims at achievement and affirmation, is always discarding something, rejecting something, demolishing something, and clearing a place for something new. It thirsts so strongly for the new that it regards everything that has already been created, everything that is old, as nothing in comparison with the new, and often destroys the old. The psychology of the museum curator is incompatible with that of the creative individual: one is conservative, the other revolutionary. What conclusions can we draw about the future of this type of ecclesiastical piety? Our harsh, stressful, and agonizing life experience turns to the Church with all its aches and pains, with all its harsh intensity. Our life today certainly demands creativity, a creativity which is able not only to reconsider and change what is old, but also to create something new, respond to new problems, penetrating new and often uncultured, traditionless strata of society. The Church will be swamped with simple people. The Church will be overwhelmed by their problems. The Church must descend to their level. This would seem to seal the fate of the aesthetic elite.

But precisely because it is select, elite, precisely because it is capable of formulating its ideas and expressing itself and considers itself the guardian of all the Church's treasures and truth, and is incapable of betraying, lowering, or changing its own conception of the Church's beauty, and is incapable of sacrificial love — for all these reasons it will defend its understanding of the Church like a fortress, it will guard the Church against invasion by the profane masses with its very life. The crowd will shout: "We are being eaten up by sores; we have been poisoned by hatred and the social struggle; our way of life has been ruined; we have no answers to questions of life and death: O Jesus, save us!" But between Christ and the crowd will stand the guardians of Christ's seamless robe, who will announce to the crowd that hatred and struggle have distorted their faces, that their everyday labors have destroyed in them that exalted gift, the ability to admire beauty.

But life itself is a thing of great beauty, of which only those are capable who have been instructed by it. Mellifluous chants, however, and softly modulated reading, the odor of incense and a blessed, somniferous atmosphere of beauty will wrap in mist the sorrowful image of Christ, will bring lamentation to an end, will cause heads to droop, will cause hope to die. For some this enveloping grandeur will be a temporary lullaby; others will recoil from it — and a great chasm will appear between the Church and real life. The aesthetically minded custodians of grandeur will preserve that chasm in the name of harmony, rhythm, order, and beauty.

The profane, on the other side, will make no attempt to leap across the chasm because they have been left with the pain, the struggle, the bitterness, the ugliness of life. They will cease to believe that with such heavy baggage it is possible — and necessary — to approach the Church. And then, within that miserable and godless world, there will arise, if they have not arisen already, false Christs and false prophets, sectarian preachers of various kinds and in varying degrees of shallowness and mediocrity — Baptists, Evangelicals, Adventists, and so forth — who will offer to these hungry people some kind of an elementary reformulation of the truth, some impoverished surrogate for religious life, some small dollop of good will and ranting hysteria. Some will respond to this. They will respond first of all to a basic human concern for their needs. But they will not be able to discern immediately that instead of true and traditional Orthodox Christianity, they are being treated to a questionable, semi-literate hodgepodge of starry-eyed idealism and charlatanism. But the opiate will have its effect. And it will further deepen the chasm between the Church and the world. Protected carefully by the lovers of beauty, protected by a sense of delusion and hatred of the world, the chasm may be there for ages.

The eyes of love will perhaps be able to see how Christ Himself departs, quietly and invisibly, from the sanctuary that is protected by a splendid iconostasis. The singing will continue to resound, clouds of incense will still rise, the faithful will be overcome by the ecstatic beauty of the services. But Christ will go out on to the church steps and mingle with the crowd: the poor, the lepers, the desperate, the embittered, the holy fools. Christ will go out into the streets, the prisons, the hospitals, the low haunts and dives. Again and again Christ lays down his soul for his friends.

What are our beauty and our ugliness in comparison with Christ, His eternal truth and eternal beauty? Does our beauty not look ugly when compared to His eternal beauty? Or is it not the reverse? Does He not see in our ugliness, in our impoverished lives, in our festering sores, in our crippled souls — does He not see there His own divine image and a reflection of His eternal glory and eternal beauty? And so He will return to the churches and bring with Him all those whom He has summoned to the wedding feast, has gathered from the highways, the poor and the maimed, prostitutes and sinners.

The most terrible thing is that it may well be that the guardians of beauty, those who study and understand the world's beauty, will not comprehend Christ's beauty, and will not let Him into the church because behind Him there will follow a crowd of people deformed by sin, by ugliness, drunkenness, depravity, and hate. Then their chant will fade away in the air, the smell of incense will disperse, and Someone will say to them: "I was hungry and you gave me no food. I was thirsty and you gave me no drink. I was a stranger and you did not welcome me, naked and you did not clothe me, sick and in prison and you did not visit me."

It is the idolatry which characterizes the aesthetic type of piety that will bring this about, for it has within it something that should serve only as Christ's outer garment, an offering of human genius brought lovingly to Christ. But when the splendor of the Church, its beautiful chant, the harmony and order of its services become an end in themselves, they take Christ's place. People begin to serve this grandeur in itself, and grandeur becomes an idol to which human souls are sacrificed — one's own as well as others'. All the ugliness of this world, its sores and its pain, are pushed to one side and obscured so that they will not disturb true piety. Even the suffering and death of the Lord Himself, His human exhaustion, acquires an aura of beauty, inviting admiration and delight. Love is a very dangerous thing. At times it must reach down into the fathomless lower levels of the human spirit, it must expose itself to ugliness, to the violation of harmony. There is no room for it where beauty, when once discovered and sanctioned, reigns forever.

And here, as a result, Christ's servants, the priests — the successors of the Apostles and disciples — are not required to follow in the steps of the Apostles and disciples and to heal, to preach, and to spread abroad the Lord's love. One thing only is required of them: that they be servants of the cult, that they be priests almost in the pagan meaning of that word. A priest is judged by how much he knows and loves the Typikon,[44] by how musical he is, how good his voice is, how coordinated his movements are, etc. It isn't important whether he, like a good shepherd, knows his flock and whether he will leave the ninety and nine to find one lost soul and whether he will rejoice greatly because it has been found.

A sinister phenomenon is occurring now in Soviet Russia. There, everything is forbidden to the Church — whether to preach, to teach, to carry out charitable works or any organized activity, or to bring believers together for a common life. One thing only is permitted: to perform divine services. What is this? Chance? Something the Soviets overlooked? Could this not be a subtle psychological ploy, based on the fact that without acts of love, without a life of open spiritual struggle, without the Word of God, our Orthodox divine services are capable of nourishing only those who are already believers, who already to some extent understand — but are powerless to witness to Christ's Truth before a secularized and God-deprived humanity. A spiritually hungry person will cross the threshold of the church and make the appropriate response to the beauty of the services held in it, but he will not receive sustenance for his spiritual hunger, because he wants not only beauty but also love, and answers to all his doubts. In this way the authorities, with their requirements, have barricaded the doors to the Church. How often it happens that, at the request of a particular group of faithful, the doors of the church are effectively locked, when no secular authority demands it, but where the cold hearts of her children fence it off from the world in the name of an abstract, measured, and arid form and beauty. In a sense it might be better for the Church if she did not have official permission to conduct divine services and instead would gather secretly, in the catacombs, rather than having permission only for divine services, and in this way ending up with no possibility of showing to the world the whole extent of Christ's love in every experience of her life.

The Ascetic Type

The ascetic type of religious life is not unique to Christianity. It has existed at all times and in the history of absolutely every religion. This by itself shows that it is the expression of some essential characteristics of the human psyche. Thus Christianity is not alone in being characterized by the presence of asceticism. Asceticism is a common characteristic of Hinduism and Islam and is present also in ancient paganism. Moreover, asceticism was a typical feature of the nonreligious milieu so characteristic of nineteenth-century revolutionary movements. One could even say that those periods in the life of the Church which have not been imbued with asceticism have been periods of decline and decay, stagnant and undistinguished. It might also be said that even periods of secular history that have not borne the imprint of asceticism have given evidence of sterility and a lack of creative talent. Since religious life demands of man sacrifice in the name of higher spiritual values, it is always ascetic. At the same time, at its deepest, creative life is also a way of asceticism, since it also demands total sacrifice in the name of higher creative values. It can be said that asceticism has never died out within the Church. There have been periods when it was dormant, when it was the achievement only of solitary souls, while the most common and the most characteristic type of religious life was actually anti-ascetic.

Bearing this in mind, it seems to follow that it is almost impossible to speak about the ascetic type of piety on the same basis as the other types which are more or less arbitrary, whereas asceticism touches upon the eternal depths of religious life. But apart from such genuine and eternal asceticism, there is another highly characteristic phenomenon about which we must speak and which we must isolate and distinguish somewhat from the ascetic tendency in general.

This special ascetic type has its roots not in Christianity but rather in the Eastern religions and has entered Christianity as a sort of a special influence from these religions, modifying the original understanding of asceticism. The difference does not lie in the methods of carrying out the ascetic ideal in life. These can be of various kinds, but all these variations are applicable everywhere and do not point to a basic difference in their inner purpose. The basic differences are to be found in what motivates an individual to enter upon the path of asceticism. There can be any number of motivations, many of which are, in varying degrees, incompatible with Christianity. There are even motivations that are in radical contradiction to Christianity. We will start with these.

These are especially characteristic of Hinduism, and on their basis the yogis have arisen. These days they sound like the fundamental principles of all kinds of occult teachings, of theosophy and anthroposophy. Their aim is the acquisition of spiritual power. Asceticism is a known system of psychophysical exercises, which control and modify a person's normal behavior and are directed toward the attainment of special attributes of power over the soul and over nature. It is possible, by determined and repeated efforts, to subject the body to the will. One can achieve tremendous psychic changes within oneself and a mastery over matter and spirit. Just as gymnasts must exercise to achieve dexterity, just as wrestlers must follow a specific regimen to develop muscular strength, just as singers must practice scales in order to perfect their voice, so ascetics of this type must follow specific directions, must exercise, must repeat the same routine over and over, maintain a special diet, sensibly schedule their time, curb their habits, order their life — and all this to develop to the maximum those forces with which they have been endowed by nature.

The task of such asceticism is determined by the principle of consolidating one's natural talents, developing them, and being able to apply them. It does not look for any kind of transcendence, nor does it expect the inspiration of any kind of supernatural power. It neither considers this nor believes in it. Above it at a certain level a curtain-like firmament is tightly stretched, and there is no way to pass beyond it. But it knows that in this circumscribed world of nature not everything is fully utilized, that there is tremendous potential, that it is possible, within its confines, to attain power and control over all living and existing things, with but a single, limited exception — over all, that is, that is found beneath that tightly drawn, impenetrable firmament of heaven. Nature's powers are immense, but even they have their limits. For an occult asceticism of this kind there exists no unlimited or inexhaustible source of power, and thus its task is to accumulate, consolidate, preserve, expand, and utilize all natural possibilities. And on this path tremendous achievements are possible.

What answer can be given to this particular form of spiritual naturalism? The only thing in this world more powerful than this is the Church's teaching about spiritual poverty, about the spending, the squandering of one's spiritual powers, about the utmost impoverishment of the spirit. The only definition of self that is more powerful than it are the words: "Behold the handmaid of the Lord." Although these words in themselves define both the essence of the Christian soul and the whole of the Christian response to the natural powers of the human being, there is no doubt but that an occult relationship to asceticism which is contrary to Christianity has been introduced into our piety by way of ancient Eastern influences, through Syria and her particular type of religiosity. There is no need to overrate this influence of asceticism on Christianity, but, nonetheless, it exists.

There is also another respect in which asceticism can cease
to be a method for attaining higher spiritual values and become
an end in itself. Individuals may carry out one or another form
of ascetic exercise not because it frees them from something or
because it offers them something, but simply because it is chal-
lenging and demands an effort. It provides them nothing in the
outer world, nor does it contribute anything to the content of
their spiritual experience, nor does it advance them on their inner
path. It is unpleasant for them to limit themselves to one particular sphere — so it is in the name of this unpleasantness that they
must do this. The surmounting of an unpleasantness, as the only
goal, exercise for the sake of exercise, is at best a working-out of
a simple submission to disciplinary challenges and is, of course, a
distortion of the ascetic path.

All of the above are mere trifles when compared with the fundamental conflict of worldview which now characterizes Christianity. This conflict concerns the most essential, the most fundamental understanding of the goal of the Christian life and divides,
as it were, the Christian world into two basic points of view. I am
speaking here of the salvation of the soul.

There is no doubt but that the salvation of the soul is the
mature fruit of a true and authentic Christian life. The Church
crowns her saints and martyrs, her passion-bearers and confessors with the incorruptible crown of eternal life. She promises
Paradise, the Kingdom of Heaven, and eternal blessedness. The
Church teaches that the Kingdom of Heaven is taken by violence, by force. This is confessed by Christians of all convictions
and persuasions. And as a result, the question of the salvation
of the soul proves a sword that cuts through the whole spiritual
world of Christianity. Here we find two completely different con-
ceptions that lead to different moral laws, to different standards
of conduct, etc. It would be difficult to deny that both concepts have notable and saintly champions, that both views enjoy
incontrovertible authority within the experience of the Church.

There have been whole periods when Christian asceticism has
been colored by one or the other shade of understanding. Both
schools have their systems, their principles, and their practical

rules. Open up the massive volumes of the Philokalia, read the Paterikon, listen — even in this day — to sermons about ascetic Christianity. You will see at once that you have there a serious school of asceticism, with a massive weight of tradition. You need only to accept its ordinances and follow its path. But what is it like? What are its teachings?

Someone who bears in himself all the stain of Adam's sin and is called to salvation through the blood of Christ has before him just one goal: the salvation of his soul. By itself his goal determines everything for him. It determines his hostility toward anything that stands in the way of salvation. It defines all the means used to attain it. A human being here on earth is placed, as it were, at the start of an endless path toward God. Everything is either a hindrance or a help along that path. In essence there are two polar entities: the eternal Creator of the world, the Redeemer of my soul, and this miserable soul of mine which must strive toward Him. What are the means for progress along this path? The first step is the ascetic mortification of one's flesh. It is prayer and fasting. It is the rejection of the values of this world and of all attachment to them. It is obedience, which mortifies the sinful will just as fasting mortifies the sinful, passionate flesh.

From the point of view of obedience, all the movements of the soul and the whole complex of external activities which are the responsibility of that particular person must be examined. He cannot decline to do them, for he is obliged to carry them out conscientiously if they are given to him as an obedience. But he should not immerse his soul in them completely, since the soul should be filled with one thing only: the striving for its own salvation. The whole world, its woes, its suffering, its labors on all levels — this is a kind of a huge laboratory, a kind of experimental arena, where I can practice my obedience and humble my will. If obedience demands that I clean out stables, dig for potatoes, look after leprous persons, collect alms for the Church, or preach the teaching of Christ — I must do all these things with the same conscientious and attentive effort, with the same humility and the same dispassion, because all these things are tasks and exercises of my readiness to curb my will, a difficult and rocky road for

the soul seeking salvation. I must constantly put virtues into practice, and therefore I must perform acts of Christian love. But that
love is itself a special form of obedience, for we are called and
commanded to love — and we must love.

That love should be used as a standard is self-evident: it is the
measure of all things. But while I love I must remember at all
times that the fundamental objective of the human soul is to be
saved: to the extent that love assists me in my salvation, to that
extent it is beneficial for me. But it must immediately be curbed
and curtailed if it does not enrich but robs me of my spiritual
world. Love is the same kind of devout exercise, the same kind of
activity, as any other external act. One thing alone is important:
my standing obediently before God, my relationship with God,
my turning toward the contemplation of God's eternal goodness.
The world may abide in sin, it may tear itself apart with its own
sicknesses, but all these things are utterly insignificant when compared with the immovable light of the Divine Perfection, while
all this world is simply a trial field — a whetstone, so to speak,
on which I can hone my own virtue. How can I even think that I
might give something to the world? I who am nothing, wounded
by ancestral sin, covered with sores because of my own personal
vices and sins? My gaze is turned inward on myself, I see only my
own loathsomeness, my own scabs and wounds. It is about these
that one must think, for these that one must repent and weep.
One must eliminate everything that stands in the way of salvation. There is really no room to worry about the misfortunes of
others — unless by way of the exercise of virtue.

That is the basic principle. In practice, you will not immediately figure out that this is how such a person understands
Christ's teaching about love. He is merciful, he visits the sick, he
is attentive to human misery, he even offers people his love. And
only if you pay close attention will you perceive that he is not doing this out of self-renouncing and sacrificial love, laying down
his soul for his friends: he is doing it as an ascetic exercise, for
this is how he will nurture, this is how he will save his own soul.
He knows that, as the Apostle said, love is the greatest thing of
all, and that for the salvation of the soul in addition to any other

virtues there must be love. And he will train himself in this, along with the other virtues. He will teach himself, he will force himself to love — so long as it does not lay him waste, so long as it is not dangerous. A strange and fearsome holiness — or likeness of holiness — unfolds itself along this path. You will see a genuine and clear line of real ascent, of refinement, of development. But along with this, you will feel a certain coldness, an extraordinary spiritual stinginess, a kind of miserliness. The other person, the other person's soul — a stranger's, of course — becomes not the object of love, but a means for the benefiting of my own soul. Such an understanding of Christianity is often the lot of strong and manly souls. It can prove a temptation for the more worthy, more self-sacrificing souls, for those closest to the Kingdom of Heaven. The temptation lies in its extraordinary purity, its intensity, in its deceptive and yet attractive type of holiness. What can one say? How can one compare one's own lukewarm state, one's own lack of heroic action with this vast and vigorous spirit, striding forward with giant steps? How can one possibly avoid being tempted?

There is only one thing that can shield you against such temptation: "Though I speak with the tongues of men and of angels, and have not charity, I am become a sounding brass, or a tinkling cymbal. And though I have the gift of prophecy, and understand all mysteries, and all knowledge; and though I have all faith, so that I could remove mountains, and have not charity, I am nothing. And though I bestow all my goods to feed the poor, and though I give my body to be burned, and have not charity, it profiteth me nothing" (1 Cor 13:1–3).

If you judge the true essence of things by this criterion, you will begin to perceive that such ascetic renunciation of the world is an extreme form of egoism, an improper and inadmissible act of self-preservation. And then there will be some strange comparisons, some surprising coincidences. For such a diametrical opposition of one's "I" to the whole world can and does take place for other, nonascetic — and even nonreligious — reasons. Are not the true representatives of "this world" cut off from the world by an impenetrable wall of absent love? No matter what their particular concern in life may be, within their conscience there always exists that impassable chasm between their "I" and the world. The more egotistical — the more "secularized" — such people are, the further removed they are from the genuine life of the world, the more the world is for them a kind of inanimate comfort or inanimate torment over against which they set their animate "I." In this sense we see that opposites do coincide. We see here at both extremes the affirmation of one's own unique "I," the affirmation of a grasping, greedy, and miserly love of one's own property, be this property what one acquires through spiritual experience of the ascetic path or through the external and material benefits of worldly success. What is significant here is the possessive and miserly relationship toward that property.

What can be said, then, about the role such an asceticism can play in the life of the Church? Perhaps this question needs to be approached from the opposite direction. The more secularized and sinful is the world, the more passionate is the desire to get away from it, the more difficult it is to love its image, distorted by hate and suffering, and, in general, the greater is the nega-tion of love in general. The more difficult the path in secularized life, the greater is the nostalgia for the heights. Today the world is extremely unhealthy and even dangerous for an ascetic who is seeking salvation. Prudence therefore clearly demands that one avoid contact with it so as not to expose oneself to danger. The fervent intensity, however, of the ascetic spirit which has been present in the human soul in all periods of history has always borne off individual souls toward those heights where they can go to shake the world's dust from their feet, performing the one task worthy of man — the saving of his own soul.

Here I would like to pause and touch upon some of the unique characteristics of today's world which make it even more unbear-able for someone who thirsts for ascetic detachment and heroic effort (*podvig*) for the salvation of his soul. There is no doubt as to the inner and outer unhappiness and misery of the world to-day. There is the threat of impending war, the gradual dying out of the spirit of freedom, the revolutions and dictatorships which are tearing the people apart; there is class hatred and a decline in moral principles. It would appear that there are no social ills that have not affected contemporary life. Yet at the same time we are surrounded by crowds of people who are oblivious to the tragedy of our age. At the same time we are surrounded by boundless self-satisfaction, a total lack of doubt, by physical and spiritual saturation, by an almost total overdose of all things. But this is no "feast during the plague."[45] To feast during a plague carries with it its own enormous tragedy. It is just one step, one hair's breadth from religious contrition and enlightenment. In it there is something of the courage of despair. And if someone happens to be there who wants to give his love to the world, it will not be hard for him to find words of denunciation, of summons, and of love.

Today, in a time of plague, one as a rule counts one's daily earnings and in the evening goes to the cinema. There is no talk of the courage of despair because there is no despair. There is only utter contentment and total spiritual quiescence. The tragic nature of the psychology of contemporary man is self-evident. And every fiery prophet, every preacher will be in a quandary: on which side of the café table should he sit? How can he cast light on the nature of today's stock market gains? How can he break through, trample, and destroy this sticky, gooey mass that surrounds the soul of today's philistine? How can he set the people's hearts on fire with his words?[46] The trouble is, they are covered with a thick, impenetrable, fireproof substance that you cannot burn through. Will he provide answers for their doubts? But they have no doubts about anything. Will he denounce them? But they are quite satisfied with their modest acts of charity. After all, they don't feel worse than anyone else. Should he depict for them the coming judgment and the eternal blessedness of the righteous? But they don't really believe in any of this — and anyway, they are completely satisfied with the blessings of this age. But this stagnation, this inertia, this self-satisfaction and feeling of well-being which characterize contemporary man is something very difficult to take into one's heart and to love, since it provokes perplexity rather than compassion. And this produces still more reasons for wanting to shake the dust from one's feet, since it is obvious that no amount of participation in such a petty life can change anything in it.

At this point there develops a particularly elevated type of spiritual egocentrism. And with it all other types of egocentrism likewise appear. One is crushed by one's own impotence; one has come to know clearly and attentively all one's sins, all one's faults and failures. One sees the nothingness of one's soul and constantly unmasks the snakes and scorpions that are nesting there. Such a person repents of his sins, but his repentance does not free him from thoughts of his own nothingness. He is not transfigured because of it, and again and again he returns to the one thing that interests him — the spectacle of his own nothingness, his own sinfulness. Not only the cosmos as a whole and all human history, but even the fate of an individual person, his suffering, his failures, his joys, and his dreams — all these fade away and disappear in the light of my own downfall, my own sin. The whole world is colored by the glow from the fire of my own soul. More than that — the whole world is somehow consumed in the conflagration of my soul.

This particular understanding of Christianity, at that very moment, demands a most profound analysis of self, a struggle against the passions, a prayer for one's own salvation. Only one kind of prayer to the Creator of the universe, to the Pantocrator, to the Redeemer of all humankind is possible for such a person — a prayer for oneself, for one's own salvation, a prayer for mercy for oneself. Sometimes this is a prayer for what are really awful and frightful gifts. And sometimes the Creator of the universe is required to fulfill my prayerful petitions for something that is not very great — I am only asking Him for "sleep peaceful and undisturbed."

Spiritual egocentrism replaces the goal of true asceticism. It cuts off such a person from the universe and makes him into a spiritual miser — and then this miserliness quickly begins to develop and grow, because he begins to notice that the more he acquires, the emptier his soul becomes. This occurs because of a strange law of the spiritual life, whereby everything that is not distributed, everything that is saved, everything that is not lovingly given away somehow degenerates, becomes corrupt, is consumed in flames. The talent is taken away from the one who buries it and is given to the one who will lend it at interest. Further accumulation makes one more and more empty. It leads to dryness, to spiritual numbness, to the complete degeneration and destruction of one's spiritual essence. A unique process of self-poisoning by spiritual values takes place.

Every type of egocentrism always leads to self-poisoning and a certain satiety, to the impossibility of any true understanding. It can be boldly stated that spiritual egocentrism is completely subject to this law. And this self-poisoning can sometimes even lead one to absolute and total spiritual death.

This is perhaps the most frightening phenomenon that can await anyone. And it is especially frightening because it is difficult to discern, because it imperceptibly replaces true spiritual values with false ones, because at times it requires that one rise up against profound, exalted, but improperly understood Christian values without which such a rising up is impossible — it requires that one rise up against asceticism.

The Evangelical Type

I will now move on to characterize the evangelical type of spiritual life, which is as eternal as is the proclamation of the Good News, always alive within the bosom of the Church, shining for us in the faces of saints and at times lighting with the reflection of its fire even righteous people outside the Church. (Here one must immediately introduce a clarification so as to prevent well-intentioned or deliberate misinterpretations of the evangelical way of religious life. Obviously it has no relation to the current evangelical sectarianism which has extracted only a selected list of moral precepts from the Gospel, added to this its own distorted and impoverished doctrine of salvation — about being "born again" — spiced this up with hatred of the Church, and then proclaimed this peculiar hodgepodge as a true understanding of Christ's Gospel teaching.) The evangelical spirit of religious consciousness "blows where it will," but woe betide those ages and those peoples upon which it does not rest. And at the same time, blessed are they that walk in its paths — even those who know it not.

What is most characteristic of this path? It is a desire to "Christify" all of life. To a certain degree this notion can be contrasted to that which is understood not only by the term "churching," but also the term "christianization." "Churching" is often taken to mean the placing of life within the framework of a certain rhythm of church piety, the subordination of one's personal life experience to the schedule of the cycle of divine services, the incorporation of certain specific elements of "churchliness" into one's way of life, even elements of the Church's ritual. "Christianization," however, is generally understood as nothing more than the correction of the bestial cruelty of man's history through inoculation with a certain dose of Christian morality. And in addition to this it also includes the preaching of the Gospel to the whole world.

"Christification," however, is based on the words, "It is no longer I who live, but Christ who lives in me" (Gal 2:20). The image of God, the icon of Christ, which truly is my real and authentic essence or being, is the only measure of all things, the only path or way which is given to me. Each movement of my soul, each approach to God, to other people, to the world, is determined by the suitability of that act for reflecting the image of God which is within me.

If I am faced with two paths and I am in doubt, then even if all human wisdom, experience, and tradition point to one of these, but I feel that Christ would have followed the other — all my doubts should immediately disappear and I should choose to follow Christ in spite of all the experience, tradition, and wisdom that are opposed to it. But apart from the immediate consciousness that Christ is calling me to a particular path, are there any other objective signs that will tell me that this doesn't just appear this way to me, that it doesn't just appear so to me, that it is not my subjective idea, not my emotion, my imagination? Yes, there are objective indications.

Christ gave us two commandments: to love God and to love our fellow man. Everything else, even the commandments contained in the Beatitudes, is merely an elaboration of these two commandments, which contain within themselves the totality of Christ's "Good News." Furthermore, Christ's earthly life is nothing other than the revelation of the mystery of the love of God and the love of man. These are, in sum, not only the true but the only measure of all things. And it is remarkable that their truth is found only in their conjunction. Love for man alone leads us into the blind alley of an anti-Christian humanism, out of which the only exit is, at times, the rejection of the individual human being and love for him in the name of all mankind. Love for God without love for human beings, however, is condemned: "You hypocrite, how can you love God whom you have not seen, if you hate your brother whom you have seen" (1 Jn 4:20). Their conjunction is not simply a conjunction of two great truths taken from two spiritual worlds. It is the conjunction of two parts of a single whole.

These two commandments are two aspects of a single truth. Destroy either one of them and you destroy truth as a whole. In fact, if you take away love for man then you destroy man (because by not loving him you reject him, you reduce him to nonbeing) and no longer have a path toward the knowledge of God. God then becomes truly apophatic, having only negative attributes, and even these can be expressed only in the human language that you have rejected. God becomes inaccessible to your human soul because, in rejecting man, you have also rejected humanity, you have also rejected what is human in your own soul, though your humanity was the image of God within you and your only way to see the Prototype as well. This is to say nothing of the fact that a human being taught you in his own human language, describing God's truth in human words, nor of the fact that God reveals Himself through human concepts. By not loving, by not having contact with humanity we condemn ourselves to a kind of deaf-mute blindness with respect to the divine as well. In this sense, not only did the Logos-Word-Son of God assume human nature to complete His work of redemption and by this sanctified it once and for all, destining it for deification, but the Word of God, as the "Good News," as the Gospel, as revelation and enlightenment likewise needed to become incarnate in the flesh of insignificant human words. For it is with words that people express their feelings, their doubts, their thoughts, their good deeds, and their sins. And in this way human speech, which is the symbol of man's inner life, was likewise sanctified and filled with grace — and through it the whole of man's inner life.

On the other hand, one cannot truly love man without loving God. As a matter of fact, what can we love in a man if we do not discern God's image in him? Without that image, on what is such love based? It becomes some kind of peculiar, monstrous, towering egoism in which every "other" becomes only a particular facet of my own self. I love that in the other which is compatible with me, which enriches me, which explains me — and at times simply entertains and charms me. If, however, this is not the case, if indeed there is desire for a selfless but nonreligious love for man, then it will move inevitably from a specific person of flesh and blood and turn toward the abstract man, toward humanity, even to the idea of humanity, and will almost always result in the sacrifice of the concrete individual upon the altar of this abstract idea — the common good, an earthly paradise, etc.

In this world there are two kinds of love: one that takes and one that gives. This is common to all types of love — not only love for man. One can love a friend, one's family, children, scholarship, art, the motherland, one's own ideas, oneself — and even God — from either of these two points of view. Even those forms of love that by common consent are the highest can exhibit this dual character.

Take, for example, maternal love. A mother can often forget herself, sacrifice herself for her children. Yet this does not as yet warrant recognition as Christian love for her children. One needs to ask the question: What is it that she loves in them? She may love her own reflection, her second youth, an expansion of her own "I" into other "I"s which become separated from the rest of the world as "we." She may love in them her own flesh that she sees in them, the traits of her own character, the reflections of her own tastes, the continuation of her family. Then it becomes unclear where the fundamental difference lies between an egotistical love of self and a seemingly sacrificial love of one's children, between "I" and "we." All this amounts to a lustful love of what is one's own, which blinds one's vision, forcing one to ignore the rest of the world — what is not one's own.

Such a mother will imagine that the merit of her own child is not comparable with the merit of other children, that his mishaps and illnesses are more severe than those of others, and, finally, that at times the well-being and satiety of other children can be sacrificed for the sake of the well-being and satiety of her own. She will think that the whole world (herself included) is called to serve her child, to feed him, quench his thirst, train him, make smooth all paths before him, deflect all obstacles and all rivals.

This is a kind of lustful maternal love. Only that maternal love is truly Christian which sees in the child an authentic image of God, which is inherent not only in him but in all people, but given to her in trust, as her responsibility, as something she must develop and strengthen in him in preparation for the unavoidable life of sacrifice along the Christian path, for that cross-bearing challenge which faces every Christian. Only such a mother loves her child with truly Christian love. With this kind of love she will be more aware of other children's misfortunes, she will be more attentive to them when they are neglected. As the result of the presence of Christian love in her heart her relationship with the rest of humanity will be a relationship in Christ. This is, of course, a very poignant example.

There can be no doubt but that love for anything that exists is divided into these two types. One may lustfully love one's motherland, working to make sure that it develops gloriously and victoriously, overcoming and destroying all its enemies. Or one can love it in a Christian manner, working to see that the face of Christ's truth is revealed more and more clearly within it. One can lustfully love knowledge and art, seeking to express oneself, to flaunt oneself in them. Or one can love them while remaining conscious of one's service through them, of one's responsibility for the exercise of God's gifts in these spheres.

One can also love the idea of one's own life simply because it is one's own — and enviously and jealously set it over against all other ideas. Or one can see in it too a gift granted to one by God for the service of eternal truth during the time of one's path on earth. One can love life itself both lustfully and sacrificially. One can even relate to death in two different ways. And one can direct two kinds of love toward God. One of these will look on Him as the heavenly protector of "my" or "our" earthly passions and desires. The other kind of love, however, will humbly and sacrificially offer one's tiny human soul into His hands. And apart from their name — love — and apart from their outward appearance, these two forms of love will have nothing in common.

In the light of such Christian love, what should our ascetic effort be? What is that true asceticism whose existence is inescapably presupposed by the very presence of spiritual life? Its criterion is self-denying love for God and for one's fellow man. But an asceticism which puts one's own soul at the center of everything, which looks for its salvation, fencing it off from the world, and within its own narrow limits comes close to spiritual self-centeredness and a fear of dissipating, of wasting one's energies, even though it be through love — this is not Christian asceticism.

What is the criterion that can be used to define and measure the various pathways of human life? What are their prototypes, their primary symbols, their boundaries? It is the path of God-manhood, Christ's path upon earth. The Word became flesh, God became incarnate, born in a stable in Bethlehem. This alone should be fully sufficient for us to speak of the limitless, sacrificial, self-abnegating, and self-humbling love of Christ. Everything else is present in this. The Son of Man lowered the whole of Himself — the whole of His divinity, His whole divine nature and His whole divine hypostasis — beneath the vaults of that cave in Bethlehem. There are not two Gods, nor are there two Christs: one who abides in blessedness within the bosom of the Holy Trinity and another who took on the form of a servant. The Only-begotten Son of God, the Logos, has become Man, lowering Himself to the level of mankind. The path of His later life — the preaching, the miracles, the prophecies, the healings, the enduring of hunger and thirst, right through His trial before Pilate, the way of the cross and on to Golgotha and death — all this is the path of His humiliated humanity, and together with Him the path of God's condescension to humanity.

What was Christ's love like? Did it withhold anything? Did it observe or measure its own spiritual gifts? What did it regret? Where was it ever stingy? Christ's humanity was spat upon, struck, crucified. Christ's divinity was incarnate fully and to the end in his spat-upon, battered, humiliated, and crucified humanity. The cross — an instrument of shameful death — has become for the world a symbol of self-denying love. And at no time or place — neither from Bethlehem to Golgotha, neither in sermons nor parables, nor in the miracles He performed — did Christ ever give any occasion to think that He did not sacrifice Himself wholly and entirely for the salvation of the world, that there was in Him something held back, some "holy of holies" which He did not want to offer or should not have offered.

He offered His own "holy of holies," His own divinity, for the sins of the world, and this is precisely wherein lies His divine and perfect love in all its fullness.

This is the only conclusion we can come to from the whole of Christ's earthly ministry. But can it be that the power of divine love is such because God, though offering Himself, still remains God, that is, does not expend Himself, does not perish in this dreadful sacrificial expense? Human love, however, cannot be completely defined in terms of the laws of divine love, because along this path a man can empty himself and lose what is essential: the salvation of his soul.

But here one need only pay attention to what Christ taught us. He said: "If any man would come after me, let him deny himself, and take up his cross." Self-denial is of the essence, and without it no one can follow Him, without it there is no Christianity. Keep nothing for yourself. Lay aside not only material wealth but spiritual wealth as well, changing everything into Christ's love, taking it up as your cross. He also said — not about Himself and not about His perfect love, but about the love which human imperfection can assume: "Greater love hath no man than he who lays down his soul for his friends" (Jn 15:13). How miserly and greedy it is to understand the word "soul" here as "life." Christ is speaking here precisely about the soul, about surrendering one's inner world, about utter and unconditional self-sacrifice as the supreme example of the love that is obligatory for Christians. Here again there is no room for looking after one's own spiritual treasures. Here everything is given up.

Christ's disciples followed in his path. This is made quite clear in an almost paradoxical expression of the Apostle Paul: "I could wish that I myself were accursed and cut off from Christ for the sake of my brethren" (Rom 9:3). And he said this, having stated: "It is no longer I who live, but Christ who lives in me" (Gal 2:20). For him such an estrangement from Christ is an estrangement from life not only in the transient, worldly sense of the word, but from the eternal and incorruptible life of the age to come.

These examples suffice to let us know where Christianity leads us. Here love truly does not seek its own, even if this be the salvation of one's own soul. Such love takes everything from us, deprives us of everything, almost as if it were emptying us. And where does it lead? To spiritual poverty. In the Beatitudes we are promised blessedness in return for being poor in spirit. This precept is so far removed from human understanding that some people attempt to read the word "spirit" as a later interpolation and explain these words as a call for material poverty and a rejection of earthly riches, while others almost slip into fanaticism, taking this as a call for intellectual poverty, the rejection of thought and of any kind of intellectual content. Yet how simply and clearly these words can be interpreted in the context of other evangelical texts. The person who is poor in spirit is the one who lays down his soul for his friends, offering this spirit out of love, not withholding his spiritual treasures.

Here the spiritual significance of the monastic vow of nonpossession becomes evident. Of course it does not refer just to material nonpossession or a basic absence of avarice. Here it is a question of spiritual nonpossession.

What is the opposite of this? What vices correspond to the virtue of nonpossession? There are two of them, and in real life they are frequently confused: stinginess and greed. One can be greedy but at the same time not be stingy, and even extravagant. One can also be stingy but not have a greedy desire to possess what is not one's own. Both are equally unacceptable. And if it is unacceptable in the material world, it is even less acceptable in the spiritual realm.

Nonpossession teaches us not only that we should not greedily seek advantage for our soul, but that we must not be stingy with our soul, that we should squander our soul in love, that we should achieve spiritual nakedness, that spiritually we should be stripped bare. There should be nothing so sacred or valuable that we would not be ready to give it up in the name of Christ's love to those who have need of it.

Spiritual nonpossession is the way of the holy fool. It is folly, foolishness in Christ. It is the opposite of the wisdom of this age. It is the blessedness of those who are poor in spirit. It is the outer limit of love, the sacrifice of one's own soul. It is separation from Christ in the name of one's brothers. It is the denial of oneself. And this is the true Christian path that is taught us by every word and every phrase of the Gospels.

Why is it that the wisdom of this world not only opposes this commandment of Christ but simply fails to understand it? Because the world has at all times lived by accommodating itself to the laws of material nature and is inclined to carry these laws over into the realm of spiritual nature. According to the laws of matter, I must accept that if I give away a piece of bread, then I become poorer by one piece of bread. If I give away a certain sum of money, then I reduce my funds by that amount. Extending this law, the world thinks that if I give my love, I am impoverished by that amount of love, and if I give up my soul, then I am utterly ruined, for there is nothing left of me to save.

In this area, however, the laws of spiritual life are the exact opposite of the laws of the material world. According to spiritual law, every spiritual treasure given away not only returns to the giver like a whole and unbroken ruble given to a beggar, but it grows and becomes more valuable. Those who give, acquire, and those who become poor, become rich. We give away our human riches and in return we receive much greater gifts from God, while those who give away their human souls, receive in return eternal bliss, the divine gift of possessing the Kingdom of Heaven. How do they receive that gift? By absenting themselves from Christ in an act of the uttermost self-renunciation and love, they offer themselves to others. If this is indeed an act of Christian love, if this self-renunciation is genuine, then they meet Christ Himself face to face in the one to whom they offer themselves. And in communion with that person they commune with Christ Himself. That from which they absented themselves they obtain anew, in love, and in a true communion with God.

Thus the mystery of union with man becomes the mystery of union with God. What was given away returns, for the love that is poured out never diminishes the source of that love, for the source of love in our hearts is Love itself. It is Christ.

We are not speaking here about good deeds, nor about that love which measures and parcels out its various possibilities, which gives away the interest but keeps hold of the capital. Here we are speaking about a genuine emptying, in partial imitation of Christ's self-emptying when He became incarnate in mankind. In the same way we must empty ourselves completely, becoming incarnate, so to speak, in another human soul, offering to it the full strength of the divine image which is contained within ourselves.

It was this — and only this — which was rejected by the wisdom of this world, as being a kind of violation of its laws. It was this that made the cross a symbol of divine love: foolishness for the Greeks and a stumbling block for the Jews, though for us it is the only path to salvation. There is not, nor can there be, any doubt but that in giving ourselves to another in love — to the poor, the sick, the prisoner — we will encounter in that person Christ Himself, face to face. He told us about this Himself when He spoke of the Last Judgment: how He will call some to eternal life because they showed Him love in the person of each unfortunate and miserable individual, while others He will send away from Himself because their hearts were without love, because they did not help Him in the person of his suffering human brethren in whom He revealed Himself to them. If we harbor doubts about this on the basis of our unsuccessful everyday experience, then we ourselves are the only reason for these doubts: our loveless hearts, our stingy souls, our ineffective will, our lack of faith in Christ's help. One must really be a fool for Christ in order to travel this path to its end — and at its end, again and again, encounter Christ. This alone is our all-consuming Christian calling.

And this, I believe, is the evangelical way of piety. It would be incorrect, however, to think that this has been revealed to us once and for all in the four Gospels and clarified in the Epistles. It is continually being revealed and is a constant presence in the world. It is also continually being accomplished in the world, and the form of its accomplishment is the Eucharist, the Church's most valuable treasure, its primary activity in the world. The Eucharist is the mystery of sacrificial love. Therein lies its whole meaning, all its symbolism, all its power. In it Christ again and again is voluntarily slain for the sins of the world. Again and again the sins of the world are raised by Him upon the cross. And He gives Himself — his Body and Blood — for the salvation of the world. By offering Himself as food for the world, by giving to the world communion in His Body and Blood, Christ not only saves the world by His sacrifice, but makes each person a "christ," and unites him to His own self-sacrificing love for the world. He takes flesh from the world, He deifies this human flesh, He gives it up for the salvation of the world and then unites the world again to this sacrificed flesh — both for its salvation and for its participation in this sacrificial offering. Along with Himself — in Himself — Christ offers the world as well as a sacrifice for the expiation of our sins, as if demanding from the world this sacrifice of love as the only path toward union with Him, that is, for salvation. He raises the world as well upon the cross, making it a participant in His death and in His glory.

How meaningful is the resonance of these words of the Eucharist: "Thine own of Thine own we offer unto Thee, on behalf of all and for all." The Eucharist here is the Gospel in action. It is the eternally existing and eternally accomplished sacrifice of Christ and of Christlike human beings for the sins of the world. Through it earthly flesh is deified and having been deified enters into communion again with earthly flesh. In this sense the Eucharist is true communion with the divine. And is it not strange that in it the path to communion with the divine is so closely bound up with our communion with each other? It assumes consent to the exclamation: "Let us love one another, that with one mind we may confess Father, Son, and Holy Spirit: the Trinity, one in essence and undivided."

The Eucharist needs the flesh of this world as the "matter" of the mystery. It reveals to us Christ's sacrifice as a sacrifice on behalf of mankind, that is, as His union with mankind. It makes us into "christs," repeating again and again the great mystery of God meeting man, again and again making God incarnate in human flesh. And all this is accomplished in the name of sacrificial love for mankind.

But if at the center of the Church's life there is this sacrificial, self-giving eucharistic love, then where are the Church's boundaries, where is the periphery of this center? Here it is possible to speak of the whole of Christianity as an eternal offering of the divine liturgy beyond church walls. What does this mean? It means that we must offer the bloodless sacrifice, the sacrifice of self-surrendering love not only in a specific place, upon the altar of a particular temple; the whole world becomes the single altar of a single temple, and for this universal liturgy we must offer our hearts, like bread and wine, in order that they may be transformed into Christ's love, that He may be born in them, that they may become "God-manly" hearts, and that He may give these hearts of ours as food for the world, that He may bring the whole world into communion with these hearts of ours that have been offered up, so that in this way we may be one with Him, not so that we should live anew but so that Christ should live in us, becoming incarnate in our flesh, offering our flesh upon the cross of Golgotha, resurrecting our flesh, offering it as a sacrifice of love for the sins of the world, receiving it from us as a sacrifice of love to Himself. Then truly in all ways Christ will be in all.

Here we see the measurelessness of Christian love. Here is the only path toward Christification, the only path that the Gospel reveals to us. What does all this mean in a worldly, concrete sense? How can this be manifested in each human encounter, so that each encounter may be a real and genuine communion with God through communion with mankind? It implies that each time one must give up one's soul to Christ in order that He may offer it as a sacrifice for the salvation of that particular individual. It means uniting oneself with that person in the sacrifice of Christ, in the flesh of Christ. This is the only injunction we have received through Christ's preaching of the Gospel, corroborated each day in the celebration of the Eucharist. Such is the only true path a Christian can follow. In the light of this path all others grow dim and hazy. One must not, however, judge those who follow other conventional, nonsacrificial paths, paths which do not require that one offer up oneself, paths which do not reveal the whole mystery of love. Nor, on the other hand, is it permitted to be silent about them. Perhaps in the past it was possible, but not today.

Such terrible times are coming, the world is so exhausted from its scabs and sores, it so cries out to Christianity in the secret depths of its soul, but at the same time it is so far removed from Christianity, that Christianity cannot and dare not show it a distorted, diminished, darkened image of itself. It should scorch the world with the flame of Christ's love, it should go to the cross on behalf of the world. It should incarnate Christ Himself in it. Even if this cross, eternally raised anew, be foolishness for our new Greeks and a stumbling block for our new Jews, for us it will still be "the power of God and the wisdom of God" (1 Cor 1:24).

We who are called to be poor in spirit, to be fools for Christ, who are called to persecution and abuse — we know that this is the only calling given to us by the persecuted, abused, disdained, and humiliated Christ. And we do not only believe in the promises of blessedness to come: now, at this very moment, in the midst of this cheerless and despairing world, we already taste this blessedness whenever, with God's help and at God's command, we deny ourselves, whenever we have the strength to offer our soul for our neighbors, whenever in love we do not seek our own ends.

Notes

1. The biographical elements of this essay draw extensively on the two existing English-language biographies of Mother Maria: Sergei Hackel, *Pearl of Great Price* (Crestwood, N.Y.: St. Vladimir's Seminary Press, 1981; also London: Darton, Longman & Todd, 1981), and T. Stratton Smith, *The Rebel Nun* (Springfield, Ill.: Templegate, 1965). For the recollection of Metropolitan Anthony, see *Cathedral Newsletter,* Sourozh Diocese, London, issue of May 2001; www.sourozh.org.

2. Soloviev coined this description of the Incarnation, God's taking on humanity (*Bogochelovechestvo*), and it has been commonly translated as "Godmanhood." Paul Valliere has argued that a better rendering is "the humanity of God" (*Modern Russian Theology* [Grand Rapids: Eerdmans, 2001]). Nevertheless the more familiar expression is used here.

3. There is an essay on Holy Fools in the final chapter of Jim Forest, *Praying with Icons* (Maryknoll, N.Y.: Orbis Books, 1997).

4. The translation is by T. Stratton Smith.

5. The Greek word means "offering" or "oblation." In the context of the divine liturgy, the term refers to the ritual preparation of the bread and wine which will be offered and sanctified and finally distributed to the faithful as the Body and Blood of Christ.

6. A twenty-two-page bibliography of writings by and about Mother Maria has been assembled by Dr. Kristi Groberg and is posted on the Orthodox Peace Fellowship website: *www.incommunion.org/mmbiblio.htm.*

7. The "thrice holy" hymn ("Holy God, Holy Mighty, Holy Immortal, have mercy on us") is sung in the first part of the Orthodox liturgy and figures in the hours and other prayers.

8. *Sobornost'* is a principle derived from the Russian word *sobor,* "council," which also became the word for "cathedral." It means "conciliarity" or "catholicity," the coming together of many to form a whole, a communion among free persons.

9. Alexei Khomiakov (1804–60) was one of the founders of the Slavophil movement in nineteenth-century Russia, which, in opposition to the liberal Westernizers, attempted to define the specifically Slavic and Orthodox qualities of the Russian spirit. It was Khomiakov who first used the notion of *sobornost'* in a broader cultural sense. Vladimir Soloviev (1853–1900), poet and philosopher, was one of the most influential figures of his time, author of major works on speculative philosophy, the philosophy of

religion, and ethics, as well as poetry, literary criticism, topical essays, and an important correspondence. He was deeply influenced by Dostoevsky, became close friends with him toward the end of the latter's life, and is often considered to have been one of the models for Alyosha, hero of *The Brothers Karamazov.*

10. The *Philokalia* (Greek for "love of beauty," as compared to *philosophia*, the "love of wisdom") is a selection of ascetic and mystical texts by various monks and fathers from the fourth to the sixteenth centuries, edited and published in Venice in 1783 by St. Macarius of Corinth and St. Nicodemus the Hagiorite.

11. See note 2.

12. *Mat' syra zemlia*, literally "mother moist earth" in Russian, is a name given to the bountiful, nourishing earth in Russian folk tales. It was sometimes extended in the folk imagination to the Virgin Mary. An old peasant woman in Dostoevsky's *Demons*, when asked who the Mother of God is, replies: "The Mother of God is our great mother the moist earth, and therein lies a great joy for man."

13. "Holy folly" (*yurodstvo* in Russian) was known from early on in Orthodox tradition. A "holy fool" (a "fool in God" or "fool for Christ's sake") is a saintly person or ascetic whose saintliness is expressed as "folly."

14. See note 8.

15. *Sobornoe* is an adjective derived from *sobornost'* (see note 8).

16. GPU is the abbreviation of *Gosudarstvennoe Politicheskoe Upravlenie* ("State Political Administration"), one of several titles of the Soviet secret police. "Solovki" was the nickname for one of the most notorious Soviet forced labor camps, located in a former monastery on the Solovetsky Islands in the White Sea.

17. Shigalyov is the radical political theorist in Dostoevsky's *Demons*. "Shigalyovism" is best summarized by the man himself when he says of his own theory: "Starting from unlimited freedom, I conclude with unlimited despotism. I will add, however, that apart from my solution of the social formula, there can be no other."

18. Russians traditionally use pussywillow branches in place of palms on Palm Sunday, which is popularly known as "Pussywillow Sunday." In Europe, boxwood branches are commonly used.

19. The Typikon is the collection of rules and canons governing the liturgical and ascetic life of the Church.

20. St. Sergius of Radonezh (ca. 1320–91), the greatest of the saints of ancient Russia, founded the Holy Trinity Monastery in Zagorsk and initiated the new "desert" monasticism of the Muscovite period. St. Joseph of Volotsk (1440–1515) and St. Nilus of Sora (1433–1508) were opposites

in their conception of monastic life and headed rival movements known as "Possessors" and "Nonpossessors."

21. In 1720, Peter the Great abolished the position of the patriarch of the Russian Orthodox Church and established a standing council (synod) to administer the Church, presided over by a lay procurator appointed by the tsar himself. This "synodal period," which transformed the Church into a department of state, continued until 1918.

22. Sketis is the Greek name of a desert in the Wadi Natrun west of the Nile delta, one of the earliest centers of monasticism and still home to a number of Coptic monasteries. Russian and other languages have adopted it as the common noun *skete*, meaning "hermitage."

23. *Starchestvo*, the institution of elders in Russian religious life (from the word *starets*, "elder"; plural: *startsy*), is generally considered to have been initiated by St. Paissy Velichkovsky (1722–94). It was not exclusively a monastic institution: any who chose to could place themselves under the guidance of an elder.

24. See note 15.

25. See note 16.

26. See note 21.

27. See note 9.

28. See note 19.

29. See note 21.

30. This is a Russian saying, used when a major disaster occurs — flood, fire, death. The intuition behind it is that by sending calamity, God reminds us of Himself and of the fragility of earthly existence.

31. The Old Believers, *Raskolniki* in Russian, caused a schism (*raskol*) in the Russian Orthodox Church during the seventeenth century when they rejected the reforms introduced rather autocratically by the patriarch Nikon. Accepting the consequences of having left the Church, they lived and still live without altar and sacraments, meeting together in prayer houses.

32. Smerdyakov, the illegitimate and unacknowledged fourth brother in Dostoevsky's *The Brothers Karamazov*, lives as a lackey in his father's house and eventually murders the old man. His name comes from the Russian word *smerd* ("churl") or *smerdet'* ("to stink"). The quoted phrase, however, comes originally from his legitimate brother Ivan, who taught the lackey his own philosophy.

33. See note 9.

34. This phrase, ultimately derived from such eighteenth-century philosophers as Kant and Burke, is played upon mockingly by the nameless narrator of Dostoevsky's *Notes from Underground*.

35. The encyclical *Mit brennende Sorge* ("With Burning Concern"), a warning against Nazism addressed to German Catholics by Pope Pius XI, was published in German in 1938.

36. Kneeling on one knee, instead of both, was the accepted military stance, eagerly imitated by boys and any other male with even the remotest — real or imagined — connection with the military.

37. An akathist (from the Greek *akathistos*, "standing up") is a special canticle sung in honor of Christ, the Mother of God, or one of the saints.

38. See note 9.

39. The first All-Russian Church Council since the 1720 reform of Peter the Great (see note 21) was held in Moscow between 1917 and 1919. One of its first acts was abolition of the synodal administration and the election of the patriarch Tikhon (now St. Tikhon).

40. The so-called Karlovatsky Church, also known as the Synodal Church or the Russian Orthodox Church Abroad, originated in 1921, in the Serbian town of Sremski-Karlovatsky, where a group of émigré Russian bishops convoked a Church council that called itself the Universal Russian Council Abroad and proceeded to create a synod of bishops. The patriarch Tikhon condemned the group's politicizing declarations and ordered it to disband. The Karlovatsky Synod disobeyed the patriarch and thus lost connection with the canonical Russian Orthodox Church.

41. Literally "Typikon-Loving Type." See note 19.

42. Mount Athos, an autonomous region at the southern end of the westernmost peninsula of Chalcidice in northeastern Greece, is the location of one of the oldest and most important monastic centers in Orthodoxy. Valaam, an island in Lake Ladoga in the northwest of Russia, is a monastic center founded in the first half of the fourteenth century by SS. Sergius and Herman of Valaam.

43. Konstantin Leontiev (1831–91), Russian writer and thinker, believed that aesthetic values were higher than moral, social, or economic values, and viewed modern "bourgeois" decadence in a way reminiscent of Nietzsche. He ended his days in the Trinity-St. Sergius Monastery near Moscow.

44. See note 19.

45. *The Feast during the Plague* is the title of a play by Alexander Pushkin (1799–1837), published in the 1830s.

46. A reference to Pushkin's poem "The Prophet," which ends, "and set the hearts of men on fire with your Word."

Sources

1. **The Second Gospel Commandment:** First published in the only issue of the magazine *Pravoslavnoe delo* (Orthodox Action), Paris, 1939. Reprinted (in Russian) in vol. 1 of the YMCA-Press edition of Mother Maria's writings, *Memories, Articles, Essays*. Paris, 1992.

2. **On the Imitation of the Mother of God:** In vol. 1 of the YMCA-Press edition, Paris, 1992.

3. **The Mysticism of Human Communion:** First published in the almanac *Krug* (The Circle), no. 1, Paris, 1937. Reprinted in vol. 1 of the YMCA-Press edition, Paris, 1992.

4. **The Cross and the Hammer-and-Sickle:** First published in the magazine *Novy Grad* ("New City"), no. 6, Paris, 1933. Reprinted in vol. 1 of the YMCA-Press edition, Paris, 1992.

5. **Toward a New Monasticism I:** First published in the almanac *Krug* (The Circle), no. 1, Paris, 1937. Reprinted in vol. 1 of the YMCA-Press edition, Paris, 1992.

6. **Toward a New Monasticism II:** From "More on the Subject of Monasticism," in vol. 1 of the YMCA-Press edition, Paris, 1992.

7. **The Poor in Spirit:** In vol. 1 of the YMCA-Press edition, Paris, 1992.

8. **Under the Sign of Our Time:** First published in the magazine *Vestnik* (The Messenger), no. 1–2, Paris, 1937. Reprinted in vol. 2 of the YMCA-Press edition, Paris, 1992.

9. **A Justification of Pharisaism:** First published in the magazine *Put'* (The Path), no. 56, Paris, 1938. Reprinted in vol. 2 of the YMCA-Press edition, Paris, 1992.

10. **Insight in Wartime:** First published in *Poems, Mysteries, Memories,* by Mother Maria, posthumous collection edited by Danilo Skobtsov and Sophia Pilenko, published by Oreste Zelluck, Paris, 1947. Reprinted in vol. 1 of the YMCA-Press edition, Paris, 1992.

11. **Types of Religious Life:** This essay was written in 1937 and discovered in 1996 by Hélène Klepinin-Arjakovsky in the archive of S. B. Pilenko. The Russian text was published in the summer of 1997 by the Paris-based magazine *Vestnik.*

    Drawings: First published in Mother Maria, *Poems,* Moscow, 1993 (in Russian).